MW00627288

A Franklin Manor Christmas

BY PAUL WILLCOTT
WITH ILLUSTRATIONS BY Walle Conoly

WORDSTRUCK PRESS
NEW YORK

FOR ANN

First published in the United States
of America in 2008 by Wordstruck Press
www.wordstruckpress.com

© 2008 Paul Joseph Willcott

Illustratons © 2008 Walle Conoly

ISBN: 978-0-9816716-1-1

LIBRARY OF CONGRESS CONTROL NUMBER: 2008926539

A Franklin Manor Christmas was first published online in 2004 by
North Country Public Radio in Canton, New York. In 2007, NCPR
broadcast a radio-play adaptation performed by Pendragon Theatre
of Saranac Lake, New York. These and other work by Paul Willcott
can be heard or read at www.ncpr.org.

All rights reserved. No part of this publication may be reproduced,
stored in a retrieval system, or transmitted in any form or by any
means, electronic, mechanical, photocopying, recording, or otherwise,
without prior consent of the publisher.

So much of mankind's varied experience had passed there—so much had been suffered, and something too, enjoyed—that the very timbers were oozy, as with the moisture of a heart. It was itself like a great human heart, with a life of its own, and full of rich and somber reminiscences.

NATHANIEL HAWTHORNE, *The House of the Seven Gables*

CHAPTER ONE

Beatrice Karen Susan Cooper

As Professor Butch Regent worked his way slowly up the hill toward the decaying hulk that was his home, the swirling snow and below-zero cold caused him to look down at his feet and hunch his shoulders even more than usual. It made him look older than his 65 years.

He heard the child before he saw her. The hacking cough and grown-up hawk and spit cut right through the whistling and whirring of the icy wind. He straightened his long body and looked for the sound. He found it leaning with one hand against a utility pole at the edge of the street. Not that the edge of the street was visible. Snow had been falling for days, threatening to shut down even Oliver's Mountain, a village that knew everything there was to know about winter excesses.

The child hacked and hawked and spit some more. It

showed red in the strobe effect of the streetlight on swirling snow.

When she'd caught her breath, she raised her face and gazed fixedly at the worn-looking man, calmly taking his measure.

"Hello," she said after a bit.

"Hello."

Not being much of a conversationalist unless he was in the thrall of one of his periodic passions—most certainly not the situation at present—and besides that, having had little experience with children, the professor couldn't think of anything to say next.

Finally, he tried, "What's your name?"

"Beatrice Karen Susan Cooper," the child replied.

The professor, being caught up in his own affairs, failed to notice the child's shivering or even to pay much attention to her racking cough. He did remark her name.

"That's quite a long name."

"Yes," she agreed matter-of-factly.

She was taken by another fit of coughing and spit more bloody mess into the snow.

Self-absorbed though he was, the old man was no longer able not to notice.

"That's a nasty cough. I don't think you should be out here in this weather in your condition. Where do you...?"

The child smiled at him in a way that stopped him from finishing his question.

"Don't worry, Professor Regent. Don't worry."

She knew his name. She must live nearby.

"Your coat doesn't look very warm."

"Thank you for your concern, Professor, but it doesn't matter."

What an odd thing to say, he thought. *It doesn't matter. So resigned. So stoical. So old.* The professor wrapped his own coat more tightly about his long, skinny body and adjusted his scarf and fur cap.

"May I ask you, Beatrice Karen Susan Cooper, how old you are, or doesn't that matter either?

"I'm seven, but you're right, that doesn't matter either."

Pulling his scarf still farther up on his face, he thought, *Just when I when I thought I had met every single impossible person there could be in this village, another one pops up in a 20-below blizzard. And only seven years old.*

He continued doggedly, "Uh, do you live close by Bea..."

She interrupted. "Just call me Susan."

Regent didn't like being told what to do. Not even a little bit. That (and a tendency to leap impulsively into impossible-dream scenarios) pretty well defined him. But for some reason, the little girl's instruction didn't bother him much.

"OK," he said.

The child looked up at him after another fit of coughing, one so fierce that her cap came loose and almost blew away. It was quite an old-fashioned cap. For that matter, everything she had on was reminiscent of clothes his sister had worn when she was about Susan's age back during

World War II.

"Well, Susan, I'm beginning to realize that much of what I'm curious about doesn't matter, but I can't help myself. I'm full of questions." He felt rather proud of himself for taking that approach. Maybe he could learn to converse with children, provided he and this little girl didn't freeze to death first.

"Anyway, where are you going on this terribly cold night, Susan? Not that it matters."

"Now that does matter, but I doubt you'll be able to understand my answer."

"Susan, I'm a professor. At least I used to be. I'm known for my intelligence." *And,* he thought, *for little else, except being peculiar and failing at things and having recently gone broke and not having many friends.*

Frowning, she hesitated a moment, then said, "All right. I'm going to a Christmas party."

"Oh," he said.

Nothing wrong with a Christmas party, unless you have to walk to it in a ferocious blizzard and you're coughing blood, he thought.

"Then let me walk you there, Susan."

"That's the part you won't understand. You already are walking me there." She paused, then added, "In a way."

"I don't understand," he said before he could check himself.

She laughed, which brought on more coughing.

He'd humor her a little. "I must be going to the party,

too, then." He was sure he'd remember it, if that were so. He hardly ever went to parties anymore. He was out here freezing in this snow only because his car wouldn't start and he'd needed whisky. Couldn't face Christmas—not in his situation—without whisky, even if it meant walking all the way to the center of the village in terrible weather.

"That remains to be seen," she said.

"Now you've lost me," he said. He thought a moment and adjusted his scarf once again. It was late for a child to be going to a party.

"What time does the party begin?"

"Oh, it's not tonight, it's on Christmas Eve—as always."

"But that's several days from now," Regent said.

"I know. I'm early." She shrugged and made a face that seemed to say she couldn't, or perhaps wouldn't, explain.

"I see. And where is this party going to be held, Susan?"

"At Franklin Manor, of course."

Behind his scarf, Professor Regent's mouth fell open. For a moment he couldn't speak.

"But that's my house," he said at last.

"I know," she said.

CHAPTER TWO

The House

The man and the girl began struggling slowly up the street. Despite the heavy snow, they could see Franklin Manor looming above them off to their right. Other houses—some quite near—were indistinct blurs, but Franklin Manor with its many gables and mullioned windows and jerrybuilt sleeping porches stood clearly visible, its outlines strangely unobscured.

The professor left off his efforts at conversation. The things she was saying were too—too something. He wasn't sure what. Maybe just too much work. In any case, he didn't want to go where her words were taking him. His life was already full of things he hadn't asked for. What he did want was to go home and have a drink of whisky and be alone. He certainly did not want to spend the evening taking care of some child he didn't know, who, in addition to being quite ill, was probably a little insane.

"Don't worry, Professor. I won't be any trouble to you."

Could she read minds too?

They kept slogging through the deep snow, one labored step following another, looking up now and then at the old house. It rose to three stories—four in places—five, if the basement and partially finished attic were counted, and it spread out almost to the edges of the property.

A few years earlier, when he'd bought it—a deteriorated pile with sixteen bedrooms and twelve baths and three kitchens and six fireplaces and an icehouse and a burial plot and more—from a contemplative order of nuns who occupied it as a monastery, it had been a personal beacon, a bright symbol of a new life. Somehow, the adventure of owning it was going to make him complete in a way he had never been.

It hadn't worked out that way. Looking up at the old house now, he saw it as brooding unhappily.

"The house would be more cheerful if you put up a Christmas tree," Beatrice Karen Susan Cooper said.

"Yes it would," the old man conceded. Nurse had been saying the same thing. "But," he added, a little irritably, "I live alone, I'm not expecting any company—your party plans notwithstanding—and it's too much trouble."

"I know," she said.

"OK, that's quite enough of 'I know.' Who are you, anyway, and what are you doing out here in this weather in your condition?" He almost added, "and why are you wearing those funny old-fashioned clothes?" but, of course, he was much too polite to say a thing like that.

"I suppose I could explain a little," she said, stamping her feet and clasping herself with her arms in an effort to keep warm.

"Before Franklin Manor was a monastery, it was a tuberculosis sanatorium," she began.

He interrupted, straightened up a bit, cleared his throat somewhat theatrically, and for the next moment or two became rather professorial.

"Yes, of course. It was what was known hereabouts as a cure cottage. From the late nineteenth century, Oliver's Mountain was renowned for a method of treating tuberculosis. Patients would spend as much time as possible in the fresh air, including sleeping out on open porches, what were called 'cure porches,' right through the winter.

"Do you see those added-on rooms all around the sides of the second and third floors?" He pointed up at the building but didn't wait for an answer. "Those are cure porches. If Franklin Manor were still a cure cottage, every one of those porches would have patients on them, even tonight."

"I know," she said. The boredom in her voice didn't escape the professor.

"Yes, of course you do. Everyone in these parts does. I didn't mean to patronize you. It's just that, I thought you might not be from around here."

"In a sense I'm not," she said.

"In a sense you're not," he echoed, shaking his head as if the motion would eliminate his confusion and growing impatience.

"No. I came from New York City, but I cured at Franklin Manor."

The professor stopped walking. He bent down so he could look into Susan's eyes.

"Is that right?" he said.

"That's right."

He reflected for an instant that he should be alarmed. But he wasn't.

"I suppose, then, that you must have been one of the unfortunates for whom the cure didn't work," he said.

"That's right."

"I'm so sorry," he said.

"That's all right. I was treated very kindly, and when my time came, it was not at all frightening the way people imagine. At least not for me."

"Really?"

"Really. Franklin Manor is a special place. But that's a story for another time. I have to say goodbye now, Professor."

"Wait. Talk to me a little more. Tell me about the party. After all, it's—you say—going to be at my house. Who's invited?"

She seemed to want to answer, but she didn't. "I have to go now." She began walking up the hill and immediately disappeared from view in the wind-driven snow.

"Wait," he called. But she was gone.

Shrugging, Regent turned and started up his driveway. As he passed under a great white pine, it suddenly let loose a huge accumulation of snow. It landed directly on his head, as if it had been aimed there. It knocked him down and almost buried him. He struggled back to his feet a little dazed, felt around under the snow for his package of Christmas cheer, and grumbling under his breath, made his way onto the long front porch.

Stamping snow off his boots and fumbling for the key, he heard in the distance what sounded like a child coughing violently. He strained to see into the storm, but all he saw was swirling whiteness.

"How odd," he said to himself. "I must be hearing things."

CHAPTER THREE

Doors

The lock in the massive oak door was like much of the house; it was perverse. When it was cold like this, it required long minutes of jiggling the key and swearing. Regent straightened up for a moment and fought for composure.

"Can't even get the front door open," he said through clenched teeth. He drifted off into thoughts of what might have been. If he hadn't started going broke soon after buying the old house, he would have hired a hardnosed general contractor to oversee a proper renovation. As it was, the improvements he'd made had been done ineffectually on the cheap. And then he'd gone dead broke, and all work had stopped.

As frustrated as he was with the lock, he nevertheless took a moment to look down the sweeping front porch. It was twelve feet deep and stretched seventy-four feet across the front of the house then turned and went down the south side for forty feet more. An antique photograph of patients lined up along it in the sort of chaise lounges called cure chairs was the first thing that had drawn him to the house. He'd never understood why that was.

In truth, "why" didn't matter. He was impulsive. He knew that. And at the time, he'd been at loose ends. He'd needed something in his life to make it interesting. Actually, more than interesting, something to give him a sense of accomplishment. Or maybe significance. Something, anyway.

The nuns he'd bought the house from had been kind and generous in their leave-taking. They'd left some furniture. They'd provided service manuals for every mechanical device in the building, from the fifty-year-old boiler to the commercial freezer. And they had assured him that they would always keep him in their prayers.

To most people in Oliver's Mountain, that last was no small thing. For years, the nuns' prayers had brought about village miracles, large and small. In the beginning, Regent did sense a little divine succor in the hard job of managing the place. But that was then. This was now.

Finally, the key turned, and he pushed the big door open.

For a moment, Regent almost felt his golden retriever, Maalox, pushing past him. He'd trot to the nearest fireplace, make two or three tight circles, and flop down on the warm hearth with his head on his paws. The death of Maalox had been harder to bear than going broke. The house was an empty place without him.

In the beginning, there would be a fine big fire on every one of the six fireplaces at a time like this. He and Maalox would sit by first one, then another. He'd have a little single malt whisky or a cup of sweet milky tea and imagine himself to be an English country squire, a man of substance gazing out the big windows onto the moors. He'd read one of the several thousand books he still didn't have shelves for.

"What'll it be tonight, Maalox? Jane Austen? Shall we check in on Lord Peter Wimsey? Who do you like, Maalox?"

All that seemed like a long time ago. Now, the house stood dark, chilly, and soundless except for windblown trees scraping against its sides.

He took off his wet boots and began a room-by-room inspection to check for cold spots or other problems. It was a twice-daily exercise throughout the long winter. But truth to tell, he might have done it even if the house had been in good condition. It was like walking the metes and bounds of his estate; it gave him a sense of oneness with it.

He'd wait until he'd finished his rounds to open the whisky. He was so broke that he allowed himself little of it these days, and he wanted to be able to give it his full attention.

His first stop was the boiler room. The huge, green, submarine-shaped boiler was full of fire. That didn't necessarily mean that heat was going everywhere it was needed though. Once, a radiator had malfunctioned and the pipes in an exterior wall had frozen, causing a great deal of expensive damage. He had closed off that part of the house without making repairs.

He moved slowly up the four flights of stairs toward the attic, from which point he would work his way back down through the house.

Tired as he was, the sweeping stairway of quarter-sawn oak lifted his spirits, as it always did. He rubbed his hand on the shiny surface of the banister as if petting a favorite cat, then gripped it and pulled himself along.

As he reached the third floor and started up the narrow flight to the attic, he felt warm air rushing past him.

He began to swear—under his breath, but so vigorously that he worried a little about what the nuns would think. An open door to the attic merited swearing. Allowing heat to escape into the attic was not only expensive, it caused snow to melt at the peak of the roof, and then the water would run down and freeze at lower points, forming ice dams that would cause the shingles to open up and the roof to leak.

He pushed the attic door shut with a bang.

He knew she was there even before he turned around. He'd been trying not to think about her. He wanted to enjoy his drink alone.

A quite small, quite old woman stood in the doorway of the one bedroom in the house that had no windows. Over a flannel nightgown, she wore one of Regent's cardigans, and she had on a pair of his wool socks.

"Even sixty years ago that door was a problem," she said, shaking her head.

"Hello, Nurse," Regent said.

For a moment or two, she looked at him, and he looked at her, neither of them speaking.

Then, sagging and looking even smaller, she turned and started back into the windowless bedroom. "Well, goodnight, Professor Regent."

"Uh—Nurse—do you ever drink whisky?"

CHAPTER FOUR

Nurse

While the water boiled for Nurse's tea "with a little something in it," Regent laid a fire on the parlor grate, keeping
it small so as to conserve his dwindling supply of wood. It
was crackling cheerfully when they pulled their chairs
close to the hearth and began sipping their drinks.

A week or so earlier, he'd been sitting in this same room
gazing into the fire, when he was startled to discover her
peering in the bow windows that opened onto the long
front porch. It was as if she was posing for a portrait and
was determined to appear serene. She'd succeeded.

The two of them started toward the door at the same
time. "You must be Professor Regent," she said.

He was reluctant to answer, lest he encourage further
questions and conversation. She seemed needy in any
number of ways, and he had more than enough problems

in his life already. Finally he said stiffly, "That's correct."

"It's important that I not be seen, so may I come in please?" She glanced over her shoulder at the street. "I'll go straight through the house and directly out the back, if you wish."

Regent opened the door.

She stepped forward rather nimbly for one so old, set an open-top canvas bag by the side of the door, made directly for the closet at the back of the foyer, and reached knowingly for the switches that controlled the porch lights.

"I hope you don't mind, Professor Regent. Let me explain."

Despite himself, Regent had to laugh. "What'd you do, hold up a bank?"

She smiled, projecting the serenity he'd noticed when her face had been framed in the window.

"No, of course not. I am a fugitive, though."

Regent no longer felt like laughing.

With a certain amount of foreboding, he said slowly, "Well, what can I do for you, Ms.—"

"It's Delia Broussard, but for years—ever since I worked here in this house back in the 1930s and 40s—everyone has called me Nurse."

Against his will, Regent felt a spark of interest.

"Well, Delia Broussard—Nurse—what brings you here?"

"Oh, if you would be so kind—I know it's a great bother—but could you let me have a look around the house? My time here was such a happy, useful time. I just wanted to see it again before..." She left off.

Regent looked at her and waited. What was she going to say? Before she died? Before her pursuers caught up?

Quickly, he formed a plan. He'd put her at ease and take her through the house. While doing that, he'd find out who to phone to come and get her. And at the same time, he'd learn something about the history of the house.

"OK, I'll show you the house. Let me take your coat."

"I'll keep my coat, thank you. I'm not yet warm."

"Well, would you like a cup of tea?"

"Oh dear, yes. If it isn't too much trouble, that would be wonderful."

He went to the kitchen, leaving her to warm herself by the little fire.

When he returned, she was sitting in the dark.

"I don't want them to see me. They'll find me soon enough, but I want to enjoy that nice cup of tea and have a look around the house before they do."

Regent returned to the bank robber theme. "Are you a fugitive from the law, Nurse?"

"Oh no, nothing like that. I just had to get away from my nephew and his wife. They fancy themselves responsible for my care—I'm getting along in years, and I do need help with some things—but I decided a couple of days ago that I'd as soon die as be cared for in their way."

She sipped her tea. "How lovely," she said, and took another sip.

Regent waited for her to continue. What was next—a

harrowing tale of physical abuse? He hoped not. One could only be sympathetic to that, but such a thing could easily become a consuming project requiring lots of personal involvement, an activity from which he was now retired.

"Throughout my many years as a nurse, I always tried to leave the patients as much autonomy as possible. For example, I made it a practice never to say, "Eat your supper." Instead I'd give them information about the importance of good nutrition in the treatment of TB. That gave the poor consumptives a small sense of being in control. It's always good to feel you're in control, but especially if you're as sick as many of those people were."

Regent nodded vigorously in agreement. He hated being told what to do.

"And your nephew and his wife don't leave you much autonomy, is that it?" It was beginning to sound like a cliché, the common story of an old person who wanted to live as independently as if she were young.

"None at all. I'm a prisoner in the back of their house. They lock me in. Won't let me make a phone call. Won't let me send a letter."

Regent tried not to let his skepticism show. He didn't succeed.

"I know. That sounds like an old woman's crazy imagination. It's true, though."

"They must not be very good jailers. You're here drinking tea in my parlor."

She smiled her serene smile. "Oh they're good. They

just aren't good enough. They view old people as much less able than we are, so they got careless and forgot to lock up when they went out for the evening."

"They lock you in?" Regent said incredulously.

"Yes."

It sounded too simple. She was probably a little dotty—seemed lucid enough at the moment, though—and had wandered off a few times. No doubt they were just trying to keep her safe.

She put her cup and saucer down and said, "I'd like to have that look around now, please. I want to see the house before they come to take me away."

CHAPTER FIVE

Hot Pursuit

Starting in the basement with the one still-functioning kitchen and the nuns' refectory, Regent and Nurse meandered slowly through the fifty or so rooms and porches. Few of them were finished and comfortably furnished like the parlor and front foyer. Some were in the same tired condition they'd been in when Regent had bought the house. Others were paralyzed in a state of partial renovation. Walls prepped for painting but untouched after that. A sawhorse here. A dried-out caulk gun there. Three-year-old piles of sawdust. Altogether, a mute, Pompeii-like record of interest and energy suddenly extinguished.

Nurse moved slowly but with surprising grace for one so old. And she wasn't bothered by the state of the house. Her eyes shone, and she had a story for almost every room.

"A wonderful thing happened out on that porch," she

said, pointing through the glass upper-half of a big hospital door. "In the depths of an Adirondack winter, two very sick young people fell in love right there. I've always thought that was why they recovered. A few months after they left here, they married."

Regent didn't see young love when he looked out at the porch. He saw cracked linoleum, windows that didn't fit, water damage on the ceiling.

"Sounds pretty unlikely—a happy occurrence like that in a cure cottage," Regent said sourly.

"Not at all, Professor. Not at all. Sick people fall in love, just like healthy people. Actually, I've always thought it's probably all the sweeter for the seriously ill. They're aware of how short life can be."

"Well, yes, but with so much death all around them and with the possibility of their own death waiting just around the corner—I should think that would have chilled the ardor of even a teenager," Regent said.

Nurse agreed, but only partially. "Of course there were times of great fear and sadness, but those times usually didn't last very long. In this house there was a remarkable acceptance of death. There was a sense of peace here. Maybe it was that way in all the cure cottages. I've heard people say it was. I know it was part of this one."

Regent thought about the nuns. They had spoken of the house in those same terms.

"Now, this room," they had told him, "is where Sister Frances died. She had such a peaceful passing. She sat here in a rocker for the last weeks of her life looking out into the maples and birches. Then one afternoon she smiled sweetly and closed her eyes. We buried her body in the little plot under the Norway spruce, but her spirit has remained here inside."

Regent said, "I suppose that sense of peace was why you were happy here, Nurse?"

"That was the most important reason. But also, I felt that I was useful here. By some good fortune, I found in this blessed place what I was put on this earth to do. I've known so many people who get nothing from their work but a paycheck. I've always found that to be a sad thing."

The professor nodded vigorously in agreement. He resisted the urge to say more. He could have gone on about this subject for a very long time.

Nurse stopped talking for a moment and turned her head to one side as if listening carefully for something. "I wonder, Professor, if you ever have the sense that you are sharing this house?"

He wasn't sure exactly what she meant, but he didn't ask her to explain, lest she go off about ghosts and the spirit world and become tedious. Instead, he willed her question to be about history and memories and the way the people of Oliver's Mountain seemed to have a sense of ownership of the house, even as he himself made the mortgage payments. Looking at her question in this way allowed him to be agreeable and say, "Sure, in a way," before changing the subject.

"Nurse, where is your nephew's house?"

"Just down by the trailhead near Merganser Bay. It's the one with peeling yellow paint in that fine stand of birches. My room is in back by the railroad tracks, and in early spring I can see the wild forget-me-nots along the right-of-way."

He knew the house. It was small, one story, frame, and except for the birches and forget-me-nots, completely lacking in charm. It was surrounded by a chain link fence and patrolled by an ill-tempered German shepherd.

"What does your nephew do for a living?"

"Nothing much. Odd jobs. Drives a snowplow sometimes. His wife is a waitress. For the most part they live on what she makes. And my little income."

So, he thought, *maybe she is a sort of prisoner. If she has a pension of some sort in addition to social security, that might be reason enough for the nephew to make sure she doesn't move out.*

They were standing quietly, looking out a third floor window onto the village below, when the doorbell sounded. It went on for a full ten seconds.

"That will be Ferdie," Nurse said.

"Ferdie's your nephew?"

"That's right. Ferdie Roscoe. Well, thank you very much for letting me be here again for a little while, Professor. It was very kind of you." She looked as serene as when he'd first seen her peering in the parlor window.

"Wait here, Nurse. It may be someone else."

He knew it wasn't somebody else. He could hardly

remember the last time anyone had rung his doorbell. He took the stairs even more slowly than was his custom. The bell sounded again.

From the landing above the ground floor, he saw a flashlight beam shining though an uncurtained window beside the front door. A small unshaven face was pressed against the glass, one hand cupped around eyes trying to see into the dark interior.

Regent turned on the porch light, revealing a man who was not much taller than Nurse. A sharp nose and bright blue eyes were inconsistent with a generally slovenly appearance and the man's aggressive behavior.

Regent neither opened the door nor said anything.

"Hey," the man shouted through the glass. "Are you Regent? You must be. I'm looking for my aunt. She's got a touch of Old Timer's, you know. We take care of her down to my house, but she got away from us tonight."

"What's your name?" Regent asked.

"Ferdie Roscoe. Hey, this ain't exactly Florida out here, you know. How about opening the door?"

"It's broken," Regent said. It wasn't entirely untrue.

"You seen that old lady?"

Regent had almost decided while he was coming down the stairs. The man's tone made him certain.

"I haven't been out all evening. How would I have seen her?"

"Well her tracks in the snow led right up this way. Then down at the end of your driveway, it looks like she dragged a fir limb behind her to wipe 'em out. You know, like a damn Indian or something."

"Sounds pretty clever for someone with Alzheimer's."

"Yeah well, she's got the kind that comes and goes. Sometimes she's smart as hell. Sometimes..." he made a circle around his temple with a gloved index finger.

"Have you been to the police?"

"Oh no. Oh no. They wouldn't be any use. They don't do anything but make trouble."

"I'm afraid I must disagree with you about the police, Mr. Roscoe. While you keep looking, I'll just go in and call them for you. I'll get the Search and Rescue people on the line too. And the Border Patrol."

Ferdie Roscoe shook his head vigorously. "Bad idea. Bad idea. It complicates things way too much. Me and the wife'll take care of this. Just like we always do."

"Have it your way, then," Regent said. "But I'm going back upstairs."

Roscoe stood on the porch for a moment, then walked slowly down the driveway, shining his light on Nurse's trail.

Regent went up the stairs smiling broadly. Smiling was not something he did much anymore.

CHAPTER SIX

Just One Saucer of Cream

When Regent got back to the third floor, Nurse was not there. "Nurse," he called. "Nurse Broussard."

He felt cold air coming from the back of the house.

At the end of the hall the window that opened onto the fire escape was open. Nurse was about halfway to the bottom.

"That isn't necessary, Nurse," he shouted down to her.

She looked up for a moment, then kept moving carefully down the snow-covered metal treads.

"Well, if you insist on leaving, at least wait there at the bottom until I can bring you your bag."

Nurse kept going.

Regent stepped out the back door just as she reached the ground.

"You're very determined, aren't you," he said.

"Yes, I am," she said. "I'm absolutely determined. And you can't imagine—well, I don't know you, perhaps you can—anyway, I didn't imagine how free it feels to find something worth risking everything for."

"Ferdie's gone now. Come back inside before you

freeze," Regent said.

"He's gone?"

"He's gone."

She let him take her arm and help her up the steps and into the house.

"What did you tell him, Professor?"

"Nothing much." He grinned as he spoke. "First let's get you warm, then we'll talk. We can go up to that little third floor sitting room in the back. It's just about impossible to see in there from outside."

Like the rest of the house, the sitting room was chilly. Regent brought her a quilt and a pair of his wool socks.

"You'll be warm in a few minutes," he said. "I'll make more tea, but I want you to promise me you won't be out on the fire escape when I come back."

Her smile told him she would be right where he was leaving her.

Over tea and Fig Newtons, they talked, but not for long. Regent was not willing to be told what to do by Ferdie, but neither was he interested in becoming instant best friends with Nurse.

He was reminded of the times he'd taken in stray cats for "just one saucer of cream," and how overnight it always became "till death do us part." But he'd take that chance again. A night or two couldn't hurt anything.

They settled her in a small, windowless room. It had been a storeroom when the nuns moved in, but when their numbers grew, they converted it to a bedroom. Regent had left it unchanged, including the monastic-cell furnishings the nuns had left behind. Nurse liked the coziness of it. And that it had no windows. It would be just like Ferdie to hang around looking in windows.

Next morning, Regent woke at 5:30, as always. And as always, he peered down from the third-story cure porch where he slept to see how much snow had fallen in the night. Then he smelled it. Coffee and frying bacon. It was one of the most pleasant aromas in the world. It spoke of fresh starts and nurturing and home. But this morning it made him angry. This was his house. He made the breakfasts in it. He had offered the old woman a bed, not a housekeeper position.

Unlike his usual practice, he took a long shower before going down for coffee. It gave him time to think about what he would say to keep this sort of thing from happening again. But then he realized he didn't have to say anything. She wasn't going to be around that long.

He had no doubt that his annoyance was reasonable. Nobody would like to have a houseguest—especially a casual one—come in and take over.

When he'd still had money, he'd thought about turning the old house into an artists' colony or something of the sort. Trouble was, that would require letting go of some of his need to control. Of course, in the peaceable kingdom he imagined, *Regent's Rules* would govern. They were the reason the kingdom would be peaceable. And he would reserve a small apartment for his exclusive use.

He didn't see any inconsistency at all between his desire to operate a communal retreat and his annoyance with having one houseguest.

"Good morning, Professor. I hope you don't mind. I didn't eat much yesterday, and I was quite hungry. I didn't mean to take over your kitchen."

Well, Regent thought, *at least she recognizes the error of her ways.*

"Can't have you being hungry," he said. It was not exactly absolution, but neither was it the angry speech he'd been mumbling to himself in the shower.

Nurse was hunched over the table—to the extent her small body would allow hunching—and in front of her were toast and jam, the remains of fried eggs, and a bowl of Irish oatmeal. Grinning wryly, Regent asked, "Did you find everything all right?"

"Yes, thank you."

He poured coffee for himself. Then remembering his manners, he looked to see if her cup was full.

Before retiring, they had agreed that this morning they would discuss what she would do next. Regent thought of bringing it up, but to do so while she was taking such pleasure in her food seemed ungenerous. Anyway, he just didn't feel like talking about it.

They spent the morning reading. He, in his large messy study—one of many rooms he hadn't finished renovating—she, in her windowless bedroom.

At midday, he knocked on her door. "Is a grilled

cheese sandwich and tomato soup OK with you? It's what I usually have."

"It sounds wonderful," she said. "May I help?"

"No, I'll do it. Won't take but a few minutes. Come down when you're ready."

They still didn't talk about her future.

In the afternoon they napped, then he went for a walk and stopped by the grocery store. Except for seeing Nurse at breakfast and lunch, it was a day not unlike most of his days in the past year or so—reading, napping, a little exercise, and keeping up with everyday needs, such as meals.

And since no part of the house had broken and thrown him into emergency mode that day, he'd had time to stare out the window at the snow and be unhappy about what his life had come to, or more correctly, what his life had not come to.

While he was out, he'd bought the Oliver's Mountain *Eagle* to see if there was a story about a missing woman. He found none. *"Ferdie doesn't seem to like publicity,"* he thought.

In the evening, Regent knocked on the door to Nurse's windowless room as he had at noon. "There's beef stew and a salad down in the kitchen. You can heat the stew in the microwave. Eat any time."

He took a tray to his bedroom where he would enjoy it alone.

"I have something for you," Liam Flanagan said.

CHAPTER SEVEN

A Gift

After he finished eating, Regent set his plate and bowl on the floor and sank back in the worn leather chair that he'd bought years earlier in celebration of receiving his Ph.D. It wasn't possible to get any closer to the radiator, so he just tugged his cardigan a little tighter. He held up the two fingers of Scotch he'd allowed himself and looked over the rim of the glass at the snow. The heavy crystal tumbler was one of only two he had left. Maybe it brightened his outlook to look at the cold through this reminder of a prosperous past. Maybe not.

He picked up *Jane Eyre*, went away into Yorkshire, and slowly sipped the whisky. When it was finished, he stripped to his long underwear and wool socks, pulled on a stocking cap, and went to his frigid bed on the adjacent cure porch.

He closed the door behind him and laid a draft dodger on the threshold in an attempt to keep the cold air of the porch from slipping under the door and into the interior of the house. He raised the several double-hung windows as high as they would go, trying not to inhale any more of the frigid outside air than he had to. He fluffed the down mummy bag once, laid a wool army blanket over it, and got in. As on every cold night, he thought of Maalox, who had always slept pressed up against him, radiating heat and calm and snoring softly.

In the beginning, sleeping on the porch like the patients had seemed a way to—well actually, he didn't really know why he'd started doing it. Nor could he say why he continued.

Maybe it was a way to honor those who had been there before him, though he was hard put to say why they deserved to be honored.

Or maybe it was something left over from his past, when he'd been seriously religious and some mortification of the flesh seemed to be just what he needed in his everyday life. He could hardly remember a time when he didn't feel bad about himself.

When his body heat had warmed the bag, he stopped shivering, and "why" became unimportant. He told himself that at his stage of life, so long as he did no harm, he was not required to have good reasons for what he did.

Around the folds of the sleeping bag, he saw in the illumination of the streetlight that it had begun to snow again—fat, floating flakes that would accumulate quickly.

He pulled the bag down from his head so he could hear better and listened for a moment. It was his favorite sound. There was no wind, and the quiet that comes with deep new snow was settling in. Soon the streets would be empty of cars, and then there would be almost no sound until an hour or two before dawn when the snowplows would begin their scraping. He pulled his head back down inside the bag, and went to sleep with no thought of the house or of what to do with Nurse or of anything that was in any way troublesome.

His peaceful sleep was not to last.

A couple of hours later, a crashing sound like a chair being turned over came up from the living room. *It must be Nurse*, he thought. If he didn't hear anything else, he'd assume she was all right. He lay still and waited, then held his watch up and pushed the button to illuminate its face. 11:45. Suddenly, light from the living room spread out onto the lawn below.

What was she doing? He listened a moment longer. Footsteps echoed from the bare floors of the almost empty room. The steps were sure and loud, not the shuffling movement of a 90-pound old lady.

He hurried down the stairs as fast as his bed-stiff, no-longer-young body would permit.

In the living room, a man he didn't know—he'd half-expected Ferdie—stood facing the big fireplace. But for an outsized head, he was small enough to be a jockey.

He turned when Regent entered.

"Hello." With a hand that was missing two fingers he pointed at a spot near the fireplace. "The altar used to stand just there, you know."

"Who are you, and what do you want?"

Regent was pretty sure he knew the answer. This sort of thing had happened before, and more than once. Never so late at night, though, and not so brazenly.

People in the village who had a history with the house seemed to feel they had the right to enter it at will. It was as if the old house was community property.

"I'm Liam Flanagan. I was an altar boy here."

"Are you aware that I own this house?" Regent asked. "I live here. You and your friends can't just come and go whenever you feel like it, no matter what your relationship with the place was in the past."

"Oh, I knew you had bought the monastery, but this was consecrated space, and whatever secular use one puts it to, nothing can change that, not really."

"Yes, well as sure as I'm standing here in my secular long underwear, the secular law trumps your sense of holy ownership. I own the house now, and what you have done is called breaking and entering." "Breaking and entering" brought Regent up short.

"Hey, how'd you get in?"

Flanagan turned back toward the fireplace without answering. He nodded his big head toward a corner of the room and said, "The Blessed Sacrament was kept there, where you've put in that curved window. And those rooms just there were the confessional and sacristy."

"It's quite late, Flanagan, and you woke me from a delicious sleep. I must ask you to leave."

"Of course," Flanagan said. "But first, I have something

for you." He held out a small box wrapped in shiny green paper and tied with a red bow. "It's for your Christmas tree."

"Thank you, Flanagan, but I'm not going to put up a tree."

Flanagan cocked his head to one side, then said slowly, "Oh, you never know."

He set the package on the mantel and turned toward the door.

"I'll say good night now. I wish you a blessed Christmas."

Then he was gone.

Regent grabbed the package and hurried after him. He turned on a porchlight and took a couple of barefoot steps out into the cold.

"Flanagan," he called out into the swirling flakes. "I want you to keep this ornament and give it to someone who can use it."

The little man was nowhere to be seen, and, Regent reflected, *there aren't any footprints.*

"Huh," he muttered. "I didn't think it was snowing that hard."

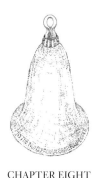

CHAPTER EIGHT

No Returns Permitted

Regent went back inside with his chin lowered and his neck stiff with determination. Even if he couldn't fix everything about the house, he *would* do whatever was necessary to get some privacy.

Tomorrow he would find Liam Flanagan and return the gift. He would be firm but not rude. Oliver's Mountain was too small, and he was too much an outsider—rudeness would be a big mistake. He would simply explain to Flanagan how it was going to be in the future regarding visitations. And he would instruct him quite forthrightly to pass the word to anyone else who might be similarly tempted to drop in uninvited and without knocking. With this picture firmly in mind, Regent returned to his cure porch and went back to sleep.

Next morning, the snow was so deep that it took the villagers some time to dig out and get the normal affairs of the day started. But it was no longer falling, and the sun was shining brightly in an azure sky. As a consequence, people shoveled sidewalks rather happily, or at least with lighter spirits than they would have on a gray day with snow still coming down. It was just the right sort of weather for the approach of Christmas, though that was lost on Regent.

He made it down to the kitchen before Nurse did, had his coffee, and dressed without encountering her. As he was leaving, he passed through the kitchen again. She was at the table then, enjoying a bowl of Irish oatmeal.

"Good morning, Nurse."

"Good morning, Professor. Beautiful day, isn't it?"

"Yes, and I'm glad about that, because I'm going out for a bit. Can I get you anything?" He'd wondered what she was doing for clothes and the like—she'd arrived with only a small open-top canvas bag—but if she did want something, he hoped it didn't amount to much. To his relief, it didn't.

"If you're going by the grocery store, perhaps you would get some Ovaltine."

"Happy to," he said. "Anything else?"

"No that's all." She reached in her pocket, pulled out some bills, and held out a twenty. "Sorry. I don't have anything smaller."

Regent fell back on old habit and surprised himself with the words that followed. "Put your money away. You're my guest. Anyway, how do you happen to have money? I wouldn't have thought your nephew would allow it."

She smiled mischievously. "He didn't. But when I was

on my way out of the house, I looked around and found some money in a kitchen drawer. I thought that since Ferdie always cashed my little checks when they came in the mail and never gave me any of the proceeds, it wasn't stealing when I took it."

Regent's thoughts moved ahead a few steps. Perhaps it wouldn't be too difficult to get Nurse into some kind of senior residence and have her checks sent there.

First, though, he would hunt down Liam Flanagan.

When Regent arrived at St. Gertrude's Church, a white-haired priest was coming out of a side door.

"Excuse me, Father. I'm Butch Regent. I own the old monastery. I wonder if you could give me a moment."

The two men squinted at each other in the bright sun reflecting off the snow.

"Ah, yes, Professor Regent. I'm Father Daniel O'Leary. What can I do for you?"

"Do you know a Liam Flanagan? He was one of your altar boys, I believe."

"Oh, quite well, quite well," Father O'Leary answered.

"He left something at the monastery, and I want to return it to him," Regent said.

"Did he now? When was that?"

"Just last night," Regent said.

"Indeed. What did he give you?"

"He said it was a Christmas tree ornament, but I haven't opened it."

Regent held up the package.

"Let's have a look," he said.

In a nest of tissue paper was a brass bell about three inches high. An inscription read, TO THE NUNS FROM A GRATEFUL PEOPLE.

"How interesting," Father O'Leary said. "A miniature of the large bell the nuns had in the cupola of the icehouse."

"It's quite nice," Regent said, "but I really must return this. Do you know where I can find Liam?"

"Well, yes and no," Father O'Leary said.

Regent waited for him to go on.

Finally, the priest said, "Liam Flanagan has been dead for several years."

"Oh. That must be a different Liam Flanagan," Regent said.

"I doubt it," Father O'Leary said, his voice heavy with priestly authority.

"I'm afraid I don't understand," Regent said.

"It's not difficult," Father O'Leary said. "The bell was important to the nuns in ever so many ways. They didn't want you to be without one, and Liam delivered it for them.

"We can talk about this further, if you like. Come back anytime. But just now, I'm late for an appointment."

Regent put the bell back in its box and for a long moment stood quite still in the brilliant winter light feeling dazed.

CHAPTER NINE

Scapular Man

It was like everything else about the house. Try to assert yourself and solve even a small problem and the small problem became a big problem.

Blinking in the bright light, Regent looked down at his feet and shook his head and stamped straight ahead on the unshoveled sidewalks.

He would do what he always did when circumstances threatened to become more than he could handle—he'd take a long walk. If that didn't help, he'd know he had a serious problem.

Not that what he faced here was a problem exactly. A mystery, but that was not the same as a problem. Keeping Franklin Manor from deteriorating further was a problem. What to do with Nurse was a problem. The appearance of a dead former altar boy was a mere mystery. Easily dealt with. Nothing was required except certain belief that there was a rational explanation for it. He smiled at the thought of certain belief. The old house had seen a great deal of certain belief. It should support a little more, even if the kind he had in mind was different from that of the nuns.

As he walked, his spirits rose. The day continued cold and dry and brilliantly sunny. There was so much Christmas cheer in the air, Regent felt like a character in a Normal Rockwell illustration. He was no fan of Rockwell—thought him treacly—but at the moment, living in a Rockwell scene seemed not wholly insupportable.

The main street of the village center was festooned with garlands. Bits of carols reached out to him every time a shop door opened.

"Beautiful day, isn't it," a wizened little man said to him. He had the look of a panhandler. His clothes were worn, and it had been several days since his face had known a razor. The panhandler effect was belied by the man's directness and good cheer.

"That it is," Regent responded.

"Pardon me," the man said, "but aren't you Professor Regent, the owner of the old monastery?" He seemed about the same age as Nurse—somewhere in his eighties at least.

Regent wondered if he might have a sign on his back that said, "Gets on well with ancient people."

"That's right."

"Oh good. I'm very pleased to meet you. My name is Jason Goehring." He stuck out a mittened hand, and the two men shook. "I've meant to come up and see you—find out how it's going for you at the monastery. I used to help the nuns with things."

A passerby touched Goehring on the shoulder and said, "Merry Christmas, Scap."

Regent's face registered mild curiosity. Goehring noticed.

"Scap's my nickname. It's short for "scapular.""

Regent managed not to laugh.

"Scapular?"

"That's right."

As the little man continued speaking, he gained speed until words were fairly flying out of his mouth. "I got the name when the nuns were with us. For the first 15 years or so, they were cloistered. Completely shut in. Never went out. Saw almost no one except priests and altar boys. The occasional doctor. They had a dentist's office in the place so they wouldn't even have to go out for that. At Mass they were separated from the public by a curtain. Spent day and night in prayer and meditation.

"Now, that being the case, you are probably wondering how they got their food and other necessities of daily life."

Regent wasn't wondering that at all. He was wondering which room had been the dentist's office. It was the first he'd heard of it. He was also wondering how he could get away from this fast-talking elf without seeming rude.

Scap went on. "Their faith was absolute. Depended on the community to take care of them. Volunteers did the maintenance. All of it—painting, roofing, plumbing, heating, broken windows—you name it."

"I'm aware of that," Regent said dryly. He'd hardly known a day without thinking about that volunteer labor. He'd bought the old house expecting to deal with a lot of deferred maintenance, but he hadn't been prepared for the crazy quilt that had resulted from having work done by every Catholic male in the village who owned a screwdriver or a hammer.

Scap stayed on message even in the absence of encouragement. "Sometimes they would run out of food. I never did understand why that would happen, but it did. And when it did, they'd ring the big bell that was in the icehouse cupola. You know, it was like a belfry. You could hear it all over the village. If it wasn't at Mass time, we'd all know something was wrong. Like I say, it usually meant they were out of food. So somebody would take some groceries up there and pass them through the turnstile."

He took a breath and swallowed. "That's why people call me Scap."

Regent had fallen behind. "Uh, what's why people call you Scap?"

"Well, see, when somebody did something for the nuns—took care of the yard or patched the roof or took them food—I'd give that person a scapular, you know, a pair of saint medallions that you wear inside your shirt to indicate devotion. I'd make the presentations whenever we'd have a church supper or something like that. The nuns hadn't been in town long before I'd presented a lot of scapulars. So people started calling me Scap."

"I see."

"So how is it going for you at the monastery, Professor Regent?"

Not wanting to be impolite, what with the beautiful weather and the Christmas cheer that was as deep as the new-fallen snow, but also not wanting to encourage Scap to go on indefinitely, Regent measured his words carefully.

"OK. But there have been times when I could have used the nuns' bell."

"You run out of food, do you?" Scap looked concerned.

Regent laughed. "No, not yet. I have other emergencies, though. That old house needs a lot of work, and like the nuns, I can't afford to do it."

"Oh, I see." Scap continued to look concerned—more concerned than Regent was comfortable with. He tried irony.

"Maybe I should declare myself to be a one-man monastic order, stay indoors all the time, and get a bell."

It took Scap a moment to realize that Regent was joking. When he did catch on, he nudged Regent's shoulder with a skinny forearm and laughed.

"That's a good one," he said.

Then Regent remembered. "Actually, I already have a bell." He pulled off a glove and opened the box. "See." He held it out for Scap to examine.

Scap reached toward the box and said, "May I?"

"Sure. In fact, you can have it. Put it on your Christmas tree."

Scap held the little bell up to catch the light of the bright sun. Then he brought it down and turned it around and around in his hand in a sort of caressing motion.

"Where did you get this?" he asked.

"From a man who said he was Liam Flanagan."

"*SAID* he was?"

"Yes."

"A little guy? Real big head? Couple of missing fingers?"

Up until then, Regent hadn't been cold, but suddenly it was as if the sun had gone behind a cloud and the wind had come up. He didn't say anything for a moment.

"What can you tell me, Scap? I mean, besides Liam Flanagan is dead."

"Liam is that, all right. God rest his soul." He made the sign of the cross.

"Then who came to my house in the middle of the night and gave me this little bell?"

"Well, Liam Flanagan." He said it with careful patience, as if he thought Regent might be a little slow.

"Oh." That was all Regent could manage. No point arguing. Perhaps even less point trying to understand what was going on. He'd just not think about any of it.

"Well, anyway, Scap, why don't you take this bell and put it on your Christmas tree."

Scap looked confused. "I couldn't do that, Professor."

"Why not? I have no use for it. I haven't put up a Christmas tree in several years."

"No, no. You keep it, Professor. You may change your mind about having a Christmas tree."

Scap wrapped the bell carefully in the tissue and put it back in the box.

"Nice to chat with you, Professor. I have to go now, but I sure would like to come by sometime and see what you're doing with the house."

Why ask permission, Regent thought. *Nobody else does.* But he didn't say that. Instead, he surprised himself by saying, "Sure. Come by anytime."

CHAPTER TEN

The Specialty of the House

As soon as Regent opened the door, he knew something was wrong. Something he'd come to call a "Franklin Manor surprise" was in the works, though there'd been so many of them, they were no longer especially surprising. He'd developed an ability to sense them even before he knew exactly what they were about.

He quickly exchanged his snowy boots for slippers and hung up his coat and stocking cap, listening intently as he did. Whatever the trouble, it was not a kind that made noise. He put the bell on a table in the parlor, then went down to the basement to begin the usual systematic check.

At the bottom of the stairs, he saw what he had been sensing. This surprise was so big and serious, he almost laughed. In the nuns' refectory, part of the ceiling had fallen in, and water was leaking from overhead pipes at several points. The dining table and surrounding floor were covered in plaster and water, and the mess was growing rapidly.

Regent's impulse to laugh didn't last long. He would have screamed obscenities, except he didn't know where Nurse was. He didn't like to swear in front of the nuns either, and sometimes it seemed like they were still in the house. So he just looked at the mess for a moment and tried to get control of himself.

"Oh Professor, I'm glad you're here," Nurse said as she rushed out of the kitchen. "I can't find but two buckets to put under those leaks. Do you have more?"

"In that storage room back by the laundry," he said over his shoulder.

He hurried into the boiler room to close the valve on the main supply line into the house.

It wouldn't turn.

Regent tried to force it, but he wasn't strong enough. A long-handled pipe wrench would turn it, but he didn't have one.

"Can you come in here, Professor?" Nurse called from the refectory. "The buckets are almost full, and they're too heavy for me to lift."

He dumped them into the sink and went back to stare at the valve. He tried again to turn it by hand, but years of accumulated rust made it impossible.

He was thinking of phoning the plumber, even though his bill was months overdue, when he heard Nurse say excitedly, "That did it. It's stopping, it's stopping."

A woman was on her hands and knees with her head under the kitchen sink. She backed out and said, "Hello, Professor Regent. You probably don't remember me. I'm Sister Julia. I was living here when you bought the house." She brushed her gray hair back from her face with the clean back side of an otherwise dirty hand.

"Of course I remember you," Regent said. "You were the one they called the maintenance nun. You were responsible for keeping the house in working order. I'm glad to see you again." Then he added, grinning, "Real glad."

"Those old pipes come apart sometimes," she said.

He was aware of that.

"I'm sure you've already seen how the joints start dripping when summer arrives and the radiator supply lines go from hot to cold."

He had seen that. In attempts to fix those drips without incurring a plumber's bill, he'd used several rolls of duct tape and a number of rags.

"I take it there's a cutoff valve under the sink," he said.

"Yes. There are others around the house, too. I'll show them to you before I leave."

The three of them watched the flow turn into ever-slower drips. Regent walked around the mess on the floor and looked at the ceiling.

"I think I see what happened," he said. "Above the drop ceiling of acoustic tiles there's an old plaster ceiling. Pipes run between the two. It looks like a big piece of the plaster just turned loose. When it fell, it opened up those old pipes."

He picked up a piece of wet fiberboard, then tossed it back into the pool of water and debris. He wagged his head slowly back and forth. "What a mess. What a mess." Alone, he might have wailed and punched a wall.

"Yes it is," Sister Julia said as she picked up one of the full buckets and started for the kitchen. He tried to take it from her, but she wouldn't let him. "I've got it. You bring that other one."

He did as directed.

"Now, we'll put this mess in plastic bags. Where do you keep them, Professor?"

For the next two hours the three of them picked up pieces of plaster and fiberboard and mopped and cleaned.

"What brings you to Oliver's Mountain, Sister?" Regent asked. He didn't bother with, *"How'd you get into the house?"*

"I have a brother who lives in the village, and he's ill," she said.

"Well, I'm sorry about your brother, but it's certainly a lucky thing for me that you came along when you did."

"Lucky?" she said.

"Well, yes," Regent responded.

Sister Julia smiled. "Professor Regent, have you read your deed to this property?"

"Have I read the deed?"

"Yes, have you read your deed?"

He couldn't imagine why she was asking him that.

He couldn't imagine why she was asking him that. "No, not really."

"Take a look at it sometime. You'll find it interesting."

"Yeah, OK" He wasn't paying much attention to her, though. He was thinking about the broken pipes. Even if he could pay the plumbers what he already owed, the cost of repairing this newest problem would be quite high. And with old brass pipes, the process was fraught with risk; they tended to split while being worked on, and problems that were small in the beginning often became big ones. He'd have to do something about it, though. Couldn't leave that valve closed forever.

Sister Julia saw him looking up at the break. "Are you going to call Thompson Bros. to fix that?"

Regent grunted bitterly. "They wouldn't come. I owe them too much money. No, I'll just do what I usually do."

"What's that?"

"Duct tape."

Sister Julia made a face. So did Nurse. It was clearly not a problem that could be solved with duct tape.

"Is the phone still in the foyer?" Sister Julia asked. When she came back, she said, "They'll be here in a few minutes."

"Who?"

"Emil and Shorty. They worked on the house from time to time when we lived here."

Regent felt a lot of different things at that moment. Embarrassed to be needy. Worried about how he could pay the men. Angry. The one thing he didn't feel was grateful.

"Sister, I know you mean well, but I have no money to pay them."

"They don't charge for their work."

"You mean they didn't charge you nuns. But..."

"I mean they don't charge, Professor. Oh, I think I hear them now."

The professor might as well not have been present for the next couple of hours. The two men and the nun took over and worked steadily until the job was finished. Regent watched quietly and became increasingly remote and unhappy. Such feelings were made more disagreeable by his sense that they were inappropriate.

When the repair was completed, the room cleaned, and the water flowing again through new pipes that didn't leak, Nurse asked if she might make a pot of tea. Regent assented but declined to have any himself.

When it was ready, Sister Julia asked, "May I say, Professor, you look pretty unhappy. Is something wrong?"

"Well, of course something's wrong," he said heatedly. "A lot of things are wrong. Isn't that obvious?"

"Not to me," Sister Julia said.

Nurse's expression said that it wasn't obvious to her either.

Regent said angrily, "This house is falling down around me, and there's nothing I can do to prevent it. In the beginning, I had very high hopes for what it would become and what it would do for me."

He paused and stared pensively into the distance.

"But all I've ever gotten from it is frustration, worry, and plumbing surprises. I tell you frankly, Sister, I would be better off if I had never even seen this place."

Nurse looked shocked by Regent's despairing words, but Sister Julia was unaffected.

"This house can be discouraging," she acknowledged. "Sometimes it seems to have difficulty built into its very foundation. But that's far from the whole story."

"Is that so?" Regent said it sarcastically and went on quite rudely. "What else? Leftover tuberculosis germs? Something like that?"

"Angels, Professor Regent. Angels."

"Sister, I sincerely appreciate your help this afternoon, but I'm very tired now. I'm going up and lie down for a while."

He left the room stiff-legged with vexation at her silly piety.

CHAPTER ELEVEN

Dreams and Plans

Regent shut the door to his room and flopped into his old leather chair like a petulant teenager. For a long time, he stared out the window at the sun setting behind the mountains. After a bit, he slipped away to maudlin thoughts of his beloved Maalox. Maalox had a ten-minute rule; anger and frustration could stay for ten minutes, and then he'd send them packing like the unwelcome intruders they were. He needed Maalox now.

Franklin Manor had been supposed to save Regent from such feelings. He had bought it after a lifetime of quixotic endeavors that had come to little except something that felt like failure.

Graduate school had not suited him, though he'd stuck it out until he'd earned a Ph.D. He'd taught for a number of increasingly unhappy years until he'd gotten so cranky that his dean persuaded him to give it up. He tried several things after that, but none had worked out. Then along came the 1990s and day trading. That had made all the difference.

At last he was succeeding at something. True, it was

only making money—actually quite a lot of it—but limited as that was, it was better than failing. Ultimately, he reached a point where he could almost forgive himself the mistakes and disappointments of his life. All he needed was an additional something that would make him feel like he was doing more than just waking up every day and adding to his net worth. That was when Franklin Manor had entered his life.

Franklin Manor was no mere parcel of real estate; it was an opportunity to redeem wasted years. In the beginning, it was not clear how the house would do that, but before he was well into the renovation process, it came to him.

He would turn it into an artists' colony, something like Yaddo in Saratoga Springs. It already had a history as a sanatorium and a monastery. He would add one more useful and colorful incarnation to the old building.

There would be suppers at a table for twenty. Maybe more. Plays and poetry readings after dinner. Fireside discussions on topics of the day. Papers by visiting scholars. A fine wine cellar in the Oxbridge college tradition. Chamber music recitals. What a life it would be.

Then the dot-com bubble had burst.

He didn't expect to have any more dreams. He was too old to take that much risk again.

He had no close relatives, and his few remaining friends were pretty well worn out by his years of disappointment and unhappiness. When he had any contact with them after he went broke, they mostly brushed off his troubles with platitudes and advice he didn't care to hear. "Things could be worse," they would say. "You've still got your health." "Sell the house and go back to teaching."

And Sister Julia had been downright offensive.

"Angels," he said aloud. "Angels." Wasn't it enough that the basement ceiling had fallen in? He shouldn't have to be preached at by some witless smiler on the same day.

His thoughts continued in this vein until there was but a small layer of light left on the horizon. The room had gone almost dark, when there was a soft knock at the door.

"Professor Regent?"

What now?

He turned on a light and opened the door.

"I was wondering if I could make supper for us," Nurse said softly.

Another test. Was there ever anyone who had such a hard time having his way in his own house?

When he'd gotten out of bed in the morning, he hadn't wanted to repair anything or clean up anything. He hadn't wanted to have a professional Christian he hardly knew show up uninvited and provide sustaining services. And he didn't want this ancient little woman to cook his supper.

All he wanted was to be alone and in control and to have his dream back.

"Would an omelet and fried potatoes be OK?" she asked.

A picture of the food formed in his mind, and the frown

divot between his eyes relaxed as much as it ever did, which in truth wasn't very much. He was hungry.

"That sounds good," he said. "Let's make it together."

In the kitchen, he found lettuce and tomatoes and other groceries that hadn't been there earlier.

"Where'd all this come from?" he asked.

"Sister Julia brought it."

His feelings careened back to the resentment he'd only just begun to put aside.

He looked at her for a long moment without speaking.

"Did she pay for it?"

"No. I gave her some money."

Nurse began cracking eggs.

"Sister Julia is gone, I take it?" he said.

"Yes. She said to tell you goodbye, and that she's going to come back tomorrow, if it's OK. She didn't have a chance to see the changes you've made in the house."

He didn't respond.

They took supper into the refectory, where a few hours earlier there had been such a mess. The food revived Regent's spirits yet again, and he actually enjoyed being at the table with Nurse.

"I don't suppose you saw anything of Ferdie, while I was away during the day?" he asked.

"Well, actually, he did come to the door, but I didn't answer it, of course."

I wonder why he didn't just let himself in, Regent thought sourly. *Everyone else does.*

Nurse continued. "He stood around in front of the house for a time watching, then finally he went away."

"He doesn't give up easily, does he," Regent said.

"Oh, he doesn't have much else to do."

"What would happen if you just didn't go back?" Regent asked. Lest she think he was offering her permanent residence with him, he quickly added, "Say, you moved to a senior residence of some sort?"

"I brought that up once. Ferdie said that if I tried it, he'd take legal action that I wouldn't like. Have me committed for senile dementia or early-stage Alzheimer's, since I'm getting a little forgetful."

"Oh, I doubt he could do that," Regent scoffed.

"He *shouldn't* be able to, but in my years as a nurse, I saw something of this sort of thing, and with the elderly— well, a contest between a frail old person with few social resources and a determined and energetic younger person is not a fair fight."

"I suppose you're right," Regent said. "At least in a general sense. I doubt it would apply to you, though." He smiled broadly. "From what I've seen, Ferdie wouldn't stand a chance in a contest with you."

"One never knows, of course. But as soon as Ferdie believes I'm not coming back, I expect I'll find out." She looked very tired.

"Well, you don't have to solve that problem tonight, Nurse. Why don't you go to bed now. I'll wash these dishes."

When he finished, Regent went up to his porch and

crawled into his sleeping bag.

"It's snowing again, Maalox," he murmured through a yawn.

And then he was asleep.

CHAPTER TWELVE

Sister Julia Insists

Regent was just finishing his morning coffee and beginning to plan his day when the doorbell rang. He closed his eyes and slowly shook his head in annoyance. He let it ring two more times in hopes that whoever it was would go away. *Must be a stranger*, he thought, *or he wouldn't have bothered with the bell.*

As it turned out "he" was "she," and she was not a stranger. Sister Julia had returned.

"Good morning, Professor." She smiled a smile that Regent didn't trust. That much equanimity and good will had to be fake—even in a nun.

"Good morning, Sister," he said gamely.

"Any more problems in the basement?"

"Not yet." *But the day is still young*, he thought. "Come in."

Regent showed her into the parlor.

"I was wondering," he said, "could you give me names and addresses for the men who did that work yesterday? I'd like to thank them properly."

"Emil and Shorty? Sure, I'll do that, if you like. But you thanked when they were here."

"That was hardly enough."

He held out a pen and notepad to her. She took them like they might be carrying the germs of some dread disease.

"Then let me suggest a better way."

"What's that?" he asked apprehensively.

"Just pass it on. Be helpful to someone in the way Emil and Shorty were helpful to you. It's a sort of chain letter of kindness thing that the parish specializes in."

He should have known it was coming. Piety in everyday life. Not that it was such a bad idea. Mostly what he objected to was talking about it. It was one thing to behave that way. Quite another to talk about it.

"I'll do that," he said. He changed the subject. "Nurse told me you'd like to see what I've done with the house?"

"I would indeed, if it isn't too much trouble."

"No trouble," he lied. "I have to warn you, though. I haven't gotten very far at all with the renovation."

They walked through the house for an hour or so and talked about walls removed and rooms reconfigured and changes yet to be made. Like Nurse, Sister Julia had a story to tell about every room. This one was where novices got their training. That one was the bedroom of the messiest nun in the entire Roman Catholic Church. And so on.

"Would you like coffee, Sister?" He wanted to add, *It's no trouble—it'll only take me about half an hour to make it.* Maybe he'd get lucky and she'd have something she needed to do—wouldn't be able to stay.

"That would be nice, thank you."

He put water on to boil and got out a jar of instant, hoping its foul taste would discourage her from staying for a second cup.

"Oh, my favorite," she said. "I much prefer instant to brewed coffee."

Regent made a mental note of it.

She took a seat at the table under the new plumbing. He slowly pulled out a chair across from her and sat tentatively on its edge.

"Let me ask you something, Professor."

He looked at her blankly and said nothing. She didn't require his assent in order to continue.

"What are you planning to do with this house?"

"What am I planning to do with this house?"

"Yes. You know, are you going to open a bed and breakfast. Something like that?"

There it was again. What are your intentions, young man? Explain yourself, sir. He'd been asked it over and over, but he still didn't have much of an answer. It should have been like playing a tape, but it wasn't.

"No, no. Not a B & B. I'm not cut out for that." He half snorted, half chuckled in a way that emphasized his point.

She waited for him to go on.

He wanted to say, "None of your business; don't worry about it," but that wouldn't do. Besides, with a small part of himself he rather did want to talk about it.

She continued to wait.

"I had some ambitions for the place once. But now, I just try to get through one day at a time without feeling too burdened by it."

"Burdened?"

He had his sanctimony meter going full speed, but oddly, it wasn't registering anything. She seemed to be merely interested rather than using his responses to make a point. So far.

He'd risk a little more.

"Well, I'm dead broke, and maintaining this old house— not to mention renovating it—is quite expensive."

"I certainly understand that," she said emphatically.

"With respect, Sister, I doubt you do. You know that something is always breaking, but when that happened during your stewardship of this building, you had the church behind you. I have only me."

He knew before he'd finished speaking that he'd given her an opening. He wished he hadn't.

"Professor Regent, you're not alone. It's only human to feel that you are sometimes, but ultimately you are not alone. Not in regard to mundane matters like roof leaks and carpenter ants. Not in regard to anything."

He fought back the urge to shout, "Give it a rest, Sister.

Keep your Sunday School piety to yourself."

Instead he said, "I'm sure you mean well, Sister Julia, but I simply do not have your faith."

"Well, maybe you should think about that. The worrying you do has not brought about a single change in this house. All it has done is make you unhappy."

"It is what it is, Sister," he said with a hard-edged sigh.

"You're overlooking some things, Professor."

She waited a moment for him to respond.

He said nothing, lest he shout, "NO MORE ANGELS!" or something similarly rude.

"We've prayed for you daily since you moved in."

He still didn't respond.

"Also, we left you with our blessing. It's in the deed. And I'll tell you something about that. It doesn't require your belief in its power for it to be effective. You didn't create this blessing, and you can't make it not exist."

"It's kind of you to say that, Sister, but unless that blessing helps me win the lottery, it's not what I need."

She went on as if he had not spoken. "There's more, too. The house had its own special and mysterious nature even before we nuns came to it."

"Is that right?"

The sarcasm in his tone didn't seem to bother Sister Julia.

"Yes, it is right. I'm surprised you haven't learned that by now. Think about Nurse, for example."

"What about Nurse?"

"You don't know her story?"

"I guess not."

"Let me tell you, then. Nurse is the very embodiment of the spirit of this special house.

"In the time of the cure cottages, there was one part of the treatment of TB patients that was just terrible. If one of them ran out of money before being cured, that person was usually turned out. Treatment continued only so long as they could pay for it. It was a dreadful thing.

"Nurse changed that." Sister Julia stopped talking and seemed to look back a long way in time.

"And?" Regent prompted impatiently.

"It was simple Christian charity. She took one of those unfortunate souls who had run out of money home to live with her. She nursed him and cared for him there without charging him anything. She did that several more times. Soon other nurses and staff people adopted the practice.

"And that was just one way in which this house is charmed. I made you angry yesterday when I said angels live here, but they do. Some of them you see. Nurse, for example. Some of them you don't see. But they are here, and they will remain here, whether you believe it or not."

With that, Sister Julia smiled and said goodbye.

CHAPTER THIRTEEN

Still More Snow

Snow had been falling without interruption for a couple of days. There had been a lot on the ground when it began, and now it was getting so deep it didn't go unremarked even in Oliver's Mountain, where heavy snow was the norm. On the windy side of the erstwhile monastery, the drifts were creeping up so high they were beginning to block the light coming in the long ground floor windows.

Sidewalks had become icy tunnels between banks of high-piled snow. Taller pedestrians were visible as heads sticking up above the walls. Shorter ones could be seen only at the ends of blocks where the tunnels emptied out into streets. The few cars that were out felt their way along slowly.

Most of the time, the force of the weather enhanced the Christmas music and Christmas cheer that floated over the whiteness. But sometimes the snow and cold almost overwhelmed the good feelings. It was a snowfall beyond anything on a Christmas card.

Regent spent much of the day glancing up from a book,

watching the snow accumulate, and trying to put Sister Julia's words and his problems with the house out of his mind. At noon he had a sandwich with Nurse, then made a small fire in the parlor. They had both nodded off, when they were wakened by the doorbell.

Regent made his way to the door through a cloud of groggy annoyance.

It was Scap. The wind was blowing snow around his head in a frigid aura, and he was engulfed in the sound of "Jingle Bells."

"Hello, Professor. Hope I'm not intruding."

"Come in, Scap, before we're flash-frozen where we stand."

Scap stepped in and pulled off his mittens. "Do you like 'Jingle Bells'?" he asked, smiling. He reached into the pocket of his worn parka and pulled out a little radio.

Regent smiled. "Take off your boots and come in by the fire." He'd forgotten about Nurse being there, or he wouldn't have been so welcoming. It would be better to keep her presence a secret until they could figure out what to do about Ferdie.

"Hello, I'm Jason Goehring," Scap said to Nurse.

"Oh, I know you, Scap. You seem to have forgotten me, though."

She left him hanging for a moment.

"You needn't look so embarrassed, Scap. I probably wouldn't have known you either, if you hadn't said your name first. I'm Delia Broussard."

"Nurse. It's you. How could I not have known?" He spoke loudly and with obvious pleasure. "My goodness, it's been a long time. I've wondered what ever happened to you."

"It has been a long time. We were both youngsters—about the Professor's age—the last time we saw each other."

Regent put more wood on the fire and listened contentedly while they talked. They went on for half an hour or so, then Scap looked around at the parlor with its new wallpaper and fresh paint.

"This was a public room when the nuns were here, so I know what it used to be like. You've spruced it up, Professor. Have you done as much with the rest of the house?"

Regent grunted sardonically and said, "Afraid not. I've started some things, but little is finished other than this room and the foyer." Then, trying to keep his reluctance hidden, he said, "Come on. I'll show you."

If Sister Julia wanted to be helpful, she could arrange some docents, he thought sourly. He was tired of taking people through the house. It was the third time in as many days.

When they returned to the parlor, Nurse had tea waiting. For a few minutes they munched cookies that Sister Julia had brought and sipped their tea in silence.

"The snow is really piling up," Nurse said.

"Yep," Scap agreed. "Plows can't keep up. Closed the highway for a couple of hours this morning. We get much more, we could be in trouble."

"What's the forecast?" Regent asked.

"More of the same. Hey, did Professor tell you about the bell, Delia?"

"Bell?"

Scap told her about Liam's visit, then said, "You still have the bell, don't you, Professor?"

Regent pointed to a shelf under an end table. "Right there."

"Good. I've been thinking about it."

"Have you?"

"Yep. You keep it handy. Liam wouldn't have brought it to you, if it wasn't special."

"Special?"

"Exactly. I wouldn't be surprised if that little bell worked for you in just the same way the big one did for the nuns. Don't you agree, Delia?"

"Sure."

"You mean, if I run out of food, I can ring it and everybody in the village will hear it and someone will bring me some groceries?" As soon as he'd said it, Regent was sorry. It wouldn't do to make fun of the old man.

Scap didn't seem bothered. "Oh I don't know if it's quite like that. But I know the nuns wouldn't leave you to deal with this house on your own without some help."

The record must be scratched, Regent thought. *That was just what Sister Julia had said.*

"Anyway," Scap continued, "if I were you, and I got in a tight spot, I'd ring it and see what happens.

"Well, I've got to go now. Merry Christmas to you both."

It was growing dark as Scap made his made slowly down the deep snow of the driveway and disappeared into the sidewalk tunnel in front.

Regent and Nurse sat for a while longer by the fire. They said little, and Regent sank ever deeper into melancholy. After a time, they had a bowl of soup and watched the weather report on television. Then Regent went to his room.

He tried to read, but his mood wouldn't let him focus on it. Around nine he put on an extra sweater plus boots and all the usual winter gear and set off for the liquor store. It was almost Christmas, and he was unhappy. A stiff drink was in order.

He walked slowly out into the whiteness, where the light from the streetlamps bounced around among the snowflakes.

Had he looked back up at the house, he would have seen Nurse in an upstairs window watching his slow progress down into the village. If he'd been able to see her face clearly, he would have noticed its expression of concern.

Upon his return, he would have seen that she was still in the window watching for him. He would also have observed a mix of anxiety and joy on her face when the sick little girl in the old-fashioned clothes appeared on the street. And her bemused look when the huge dump of snow fell out of the white pine and knocked him down.

That little avalanche falling on his head must have affected his mind. He could think of no other reason why he would have asked Nurse to join him for a drink. He had dearly wanted to be alone for a while. But he had invited her, and she'd accepted, and the fire was crackling cheerfully, and the record-setting snow was still falling.

The whisky brought color to their faces and made them talkative.

"This snow keeps up, I may have to ring the bell, like Scap suggested," Regent said. He laughed a little as he said it. "Maybe get somebody up here to dig us out." He raised his eyes from the fire and glanced at Nurse.

Nurse looked out the window and said, "You may have to, indeed." She didn't laugh.

"Where do you suppose Scap got such an idea? Why is he so ready to believe that Liam Flanagan came back from the dead to give me that bell?"

"I suppose he's just like anyone else," she said. "His experiences in life set the limits for what he thinks is possible or not possible."

"And what experiences could he have had that make him believe easily that a dead altar boy brought me a magic bell?" Regent said.

She dodged the question as adroitly as a politician. "Maybe your view is different from his because of the way you describe what happened. In any case the important part of what Scap said to you is that help is available and that it's in the essential nature of this house. It doesn't matter whether you were visited by the long-dead Liam Flanagan, or there is some more workaday explanation that applies."

Regent opened the box and took out the bell. He turned it around and around in his hand examining it with care.

Then he put the bell back in the box, and they retired.

"It's still snowing, Maalox," Regent said as he settled into his mummy bag.

CHAPTER FOURTEEN

Sleuthing

When Regent woke, he remained motionless in the warm depths of his down bag. Even with his eyes purposely shut, he could tell that the weather had not changed. It was quiet in the way that only happens when deep snow is growing still deeper. The only sound was the occasional scraping of a plow. If the snow had stopped, some cars would be moving. He opened his eyes and confirmed what his ears had told him. Fat, heavy flakes were still coming down, thick and determined.

A few days earlier, it had been welcome. It had seemed appropriate for the approach of Christmas, but too much was too much, whatever the season.

And, that was only one of the things that was annoying him.

It was making him angry to be told that he'd been visited by a dead man. As soon as the local history center at the library was open, he would put that notion to rest.

That wasn't all that was bothering him either.

As he drank coffee and watched the clock, he dug out

the deed to Franklin Manor. He ran his finger down the page quickly, skipping over the boilerplate. It was fairly long, so he had time to build up some certainty that the special clause—the "blessing clause" Sister Julia had called it—was not there. Not that it would make any difference—either way.

Then, there it was.

The starkness of the language got his attention. He had reservations, but he couldn't help being moved by the nun's generous intentions.

"For the general well-being of Buyer, necessary succor in time of need, and the continuing peace of Franklin Manor, Sellers convey all resident angels and promise to pray in perpetuity for Buyer and house."

He thought about it as he walked to the library.

Their good intentions aside, Regent was annoyed. It was as if they'd found a way to keep an interest in the place after he had bought it. His idea of a real estate transaction was that the buyer paid and the seller sold and the seller detached himself from the property and went on to a new life. If one believed in angels in the way the nuns did, the blessing clause amounted to their leaving behind something personal, something over which he would have no control. He didn't like that. As he thought about it, he wasn't even sure he liked having them pray for him and his Franklin Manor life.

Regent entered the library a few minutes after it opened.

"Merry Christmas," the librarian said. "Snowing out

there, isn't it?"

Regent managed to say, "Yes, it is," without commenting on the woman's lack of conversational gifts.

"Can I help you with something?"

"I hope so. I'm looking for information about people named Liam Flanagan who have lived around here during the last fifty years. Where should I start?"

"Can you tell me a little more?"

"Not much." *How much more did she need?* The name alone seemed sufficient to him. "I know that there was a Liam Flanagan who was an altar boy at the former monastery. I'm Butch Regent, by the way. I bought the monastery from the nuns. Finding out about Flanagan is part of my general curiosity about the place. It's a little hard to explain."

"Why don't you do this, Professor Regent? Over on that shelf are telephone directories from the last several decades. You check those, and I'll see what else I can find."

It turned out that there had always been a number of Flanagans in the area, but only one Liam Flanagan was listed. And no Liam Flanagan at all during the last several years. Regent was wondering whether it was worth his while to contact the two "L. Flanagans" in the current book, when the librarian brought him two large folders.

"Perhaps you'll find this material helpful. I should think it would be interesting, if nothing else. One of these has information about Franklin Manor when it was a cure cottage. The other contains odd bits and pieces about the monastery."

He started with the cure cottage folder. There was an advertising brochure from the twenties, a newspaper story about a state politician of some renown who had been a patient, and information about cure cottages in general. Candid photographs from someone's scrapbook showed the front porch in cold weather with blanket-swaddled patients in cure chairs—a popular shot of cure cottages, since it demonstrated the essence of the cure. A picture from the early forties showed staff posed on the front steps in a group portrait. Front row, third from the right was Delia Broussard. He made a copy for her, and turned his attention to the other folder.

The visit of a bishop to the monastery was very big news. Apparently, every time one crossed the county line, a photographer and reporter were there to cover the momentous event. In the early days, when the nuns were still cloistered, the bishops were usually photographed in the front yard with the big house in the background.

Then, after the Second Vatican Council when the monastery ceased to be a strictly secluded cloister, it seemed that the nuns—some of them at least—fairly burst out of the building and into the public eye and the camera's lens.

As he was turning through the material, Regent glanced across the room and saw the librarian talking to a middle-aged man in a bow tie. They looked toward Regent and pointed with their heads as if they were talking about him.

After a bit of that, they walked to his table.

"Professor Regent, this is Preston Butcher. He may be able to help you."

"It happens I knew Liam Flanagan," Butcher said. "We were altar boys together."

"Well, what can you tell me about him, Mr. Butcher?"

"Quite a lot, actually. Not only were we boyhood friends, I did a little legal work for him. What do you want to know?"

"Actually, I'm trying to unravel a mistaken identity problem. I wonder—do you know if there is a Liam Flanagan living around here now?"

"Not that I'm aware of. And I think I know all the Flanagans. We're distantly related, and I keep up."

"Well, tell me this. Can you think of any reason why someone would pretend to be the Liam Flanagan who was once a monastery altar boy?"

"No, I can't."

The librarian returned bearing an old newspaper.

"Mr. Butcher gave me the date of Liam's death, so I was able to get you this obituary."

A quick glance at the clipping and Regent's face went pale. There was a photograph with the story. There could be no doubt. It *was* the person who had left the bell.

"Is something wrong, Professor?" Butcher asked.

"Yes, there is. A couple of days ago this dead man appeared inside my house in the middle of the night and gave me a present. What am I supposed to make of it?"

"Oh I see." Butcher smiled and nodded understandingly. "I take it this is the first such mystery you've experienced in the house?"

"It's the first such mystery I've experienced in any house." Regent said it more loudly than was appropriate in a library.

"Well, you may as well get used to it, Professor. That's how Franklin Manor is. Always has been."

"Is that right?" Regent said sarcastically.

"Yes it is," Butcher said, smiling and unperturbed. "I own a former monastery, myself. There used to be a number of them in the North Country, you know. As fewer women have become nuns in recent years, the church has consolidated the smallest groups and sold the buildings. When I had an opportunity to buy one, I jumped at it. I would have bought Franklin Manor, if I'd had the money."

"What's so special about owning a former monastery?"

"By now, I should think you would know, Professor."

"Well I don't, so why don't you tell me." Regent was advancing from sarcasm to full-blown surliness.

"I own a number of apartments and rent houses, but only one monastery. The other properties are just structures. The former monastery is a peaceful building."

"Is that right?" Regent realized he'd just said that.

Butcher continued, unperturbed.

"And your building is doubly enchanted by virtue of its special history as a cure cottage. It was famous for the kindness of the staff, especially a nurse named Broussard, who..." Regent stopped listening—he'd heard it before. He was trying to figure out how to extricate himself without being rude, when suddenly the lights went out and the copy machine and computers stopped humming. All heads came up, and for a moment everyone looked out from semidarkness into the dim light of the heavily falling snow.

Preston Butcher rushed to a window.

"Power outage," he said. "It's off everywhere." The library patrons spilled out the door like firemen, donning clothes as they went.

The temperature was below zero, so it wouldn't take long. In a few hours, pipes all over the village would be frozen.

"You'd better go see about your monastery, Professor," Butcher said.

Regent didn't need reminding.

CHAPTER FIFTEEN

Freeze-Up

On the street outside the library, the cheerful Christmas
bustle had become distorted. Carols went unheard, and
people cattled up in small groups, looking tentative, trying
to decide how much alarm was appropriate.

"What's going on?" Regent asked someone.

The man shrugged. "Maybe there's a line down."

Since no lights were visible anywhere—not in the
immediate area, not on the hillsides in the distance—
Regent heard that as wishful thinking. A downed line
wouldn't cut off power to the whole village.

At the service station a man was pulling a starter rope on
a generator that would provide power to the gasoline pumps.

Near the station, Regent saw Scap standing with his
little "Jingle Bells" radio held against his ear. He nodded
and silently mouthed, "Professor."

"Hi, Scap. What's going on?"

Scap raised an index finger. "Hold on." After a moment, he said, "Power is off in most of three counties. The snow has somehow knocked out the big Niagara Mohawk power plant at Jorry's Landing. The official temperature is now minus 7. Supposed to get a lot colder tonight." He reported this cheerfully, as if he was talking about something of passing interest but little significance.

Regent, on the other hand, exploded in a string of expletives and tried to walk a little faster through the ever-deepening snow.

At home, he found Nurse in the dim interior light putting wood onto the grate in the parlor fireplace.

"Hello, Professor. If the power is going to be off long, I thought you'd want to get these fires going. Do you have some more wood?"

"Yeah. And if the reports are correct, we are going to need it all."

He spent the next half-hour carrying wood in. Nurse went around behind him and lit a blaze in all the fireplaces. There were four on the ground floor, and two upstairs in bedrooms. Occasionally, when Regent had first owned the house and still had money, he would light all the fires at once. Despite the circumstances, it felt good to be doing it again.

The snow was coming down so heavily that it turned the mid-day light to something like dusk. Except around the fireplaces, the house was almost dark.

"Do you have any candles?" Nurse asked.

Regent gave a sardonic little chuckle. He had several boxes of dripless beeswax tapers, bought earlier in anticipation of much entertaining. "They're in the pantry," he said.

He remained in the living room staring into the big fireplace. He tried not to think about how most of the heat from the open fires was going up the chimney. Instead, he worked to form a picture in his mind of where the plumbing was vis-à-vis the fires. There was a lot of it in the walls of the parlor, so the fire there would help. The big living room fire would be less effective. The heat from it would push out over the hearth and warm the immediate area, but it would quickly dissipate in the large open space.

He found batteries for a seldom-used radio and turned it on. The news was not encouraging. There had been an electrical short that had caused something serious to happen and then, etc., etc., and—the important part—"power will be off indefinitely—likely days rather than hours. Stay tuned to North Country Public Radio for updates."

"Oh my," Nurse said.

Regent didn't respond. He walked slowly into the parlor, sat down heavily in a faded chair near the fire, and slipped into hopelessness.

"You look awfully sad, Professor. I'm sorry to see that."

"How would you expect me to look?" He said it very softly, straining not to lose his temper.

"The situation is quite threatening, isn't it," she said.

"Still, I've seen this happen a couple of times. In both cases, the damage was extensive. But then, after a couple of years, repairs had been made, and things were back to where they were before."

By dipping deeply into his reservoir of good manners, Regent managed not to be rude. He kept his eyes focussed on the fire and said nothing.

"It's funny..." she said, and broke off.

He took his eyes from the fire and glanced over at her. "What's funny?" he asked wearily.

"Well, one should be thinking of the important problems this presents—burst pipes especially—but all I can manage to think about is how nice it would be to have a cup of tea with buttered toast and jam. Perhaps that would make us feel better. Shall I make some?"

He looked up and saw the parlor and the empty living room in an unexpected way. There were candles all around, a cheerful fire on every hearth, and the snow falling outside the big windows was as dramatic and lovely as always.

"Yes, of course, let's do have tea. The house isn't going to freeze up in the next half hour." He smiled, and together they went down to the kitchen.

Afterward, as she cleared cups and saucers from the parlor, Regent turned to thinking around the edges of solutions.

He had insurance, of course, but it was unlikely to cover the huge repair costs he might be about to face. Coverage on the house was based on market value, and that was only a fraction of replacement cost. Anyway, even if the insurance company wrote him a check for the full replacement cost and more, it would be virtually impossible to make the house what it was before the damage. The 1890s craftmanship that went into its construction hardly existed anymore.

If most of the pipes froze, his only practical course would be to take what the insurance paid and sell the old house for its salvage value.

As he thought about it, he realized that as discouraged as he'd been about renovating the place and keeping his vague dream alive, he still hadn't given up on it.

Nurse took a seat beside him and joined him in staring into the fire.

"I was thinking, Professor. Shouldn't we start draining the pipes?"

"What?" It took him a moment to come back from where he'd gone and understand what she was talking about.

"You know, drain the pipes. If the power is going to be off a long time, maybe we could do what people do with unwinterized camps at the end of summer."

It was such a big house, that seemed impractical, maybe even impossible, since he didn't really know how. But then, they could start and see where it took them. They might not be able to empty every drop of water from the house, but they could get some of it out. And having water running through the pipes would slow the rate at which it froze in the domestic supply lines. It wouldn't affect the heating system though.

"It's worth a try, I guess," he said. "If you are up to it, why don't you go around the house and open all the taps. While you're doing that, I'll try again to close the main valve that controls the water supply into the house."

Nurse went to the third floor, and he began working on the rusty valve with a wire brush. He stopped every few minutes and tried to turn it.

Moving the brush back and forth gave him something to do while he worried and thought about problems yet to come. Even if he succeeded in shutting off the supply of water into the house, draining the heating system was far more challenging than what people did in their small summer houses. He didn't have any idea how to do it, and besides that, the system was huge. There were more than fifty radiators, holding hundreds of gallons of water. A few hours earlier it had been hot water. Now at best it was warm.

He took a break and went to find Nurse. "Would you phone the heating oil people and see if they can come over and show me how to drain the system? I'll be very surprised if you can get through to them, but try it anyway, please."

He went back to brushing rust. If she did get through, maybe her long life in the village would give her some leverage. He owed them so much money, they probably wouldn't come if he made the request.

After Regent had spent another half-hour with the wire brush, Nurse reported that she'd gotten nothing but a busy signal.

Regent noticed that she'd put on her coat, and he realized that even hard as he was working, he too was getting chilled.

He put the brush down, stood up from his low stool, and straightened his long body. They went into the kitchen and had another cup of tea, standing close to the slight warmth of the stove burners.

Not even Nurse was able to come up with another encouraging idea. They were at the point where there was nothing for it but to continue brushing rust and punching numbers into the phone and trying not to give up all hope.

After a time, Regent took another break from the wire brush and went to the woodpile. It was good to be out of the basement for a time, cold as it was outside. At least he was using different muscles. He was getting very tired.

The pile was noticeably smaller that it had been a few hours earlier. He'd been saving it for two seasons, so it was quite dry, and it burned quickly. There was enough to last only another hour or so.

With the snow falling so heavily, dusk came early. As the already slight light began to fade completely, so did Regent's hope.

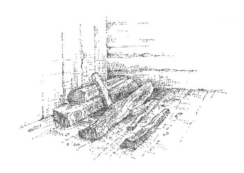

CHAPTER SIXTEEN

"Merry Christmas, Ferdie."

The clumping on the stairs almost didn't penetrate Regent's hopelessness, but he came to life when Scap entered the boiler room accompanied by the two men Sister Julia had called in to help when the refectory pipes had burst. They wore insulated coveralls, and their heads and shoulders were covered with snow.

Regent grinned wryly and said, "Maybe you guys should just move in with me. It would save you commuting time." For some reason, it was as close as he could get to saying thank you.

The one named Emil carried a long-handled pipe wrench.

"I see you already got your taps open," he said. "So now let's cut off the flow." He got purchase with the wrench and, grunting dramatically, gave it a pull. "That should do it."

The other man—Shorty—had run a hose into the floor

drain from a tap near the boiler.

"That's from one zone of the heating system," he said, pointing at the water running into the drain. "If I remember correctly, there are four zones." He shined a flashlight up into a web of overhead pipes that Regent had always found impenetrably complex. "Yep. There are the circulators."

They stood quietly for a moment listening to the gurgling water. Regent felt like an outsider.

After a time, he remembered his manners. "Why don't I make some coffee?"

He looked around and found a cafetierre. He liked to use it under any circumstances, and since it required no electricity, it was just the ticket now. He left Nurse to watch it and went back to the boiler room.

"How long will that take," Regent asked, gesturing at the drain with his head.

Shorty said, "Can't say for sure. A few hours. Maybe more. It takes a long time for all the water to make its way down out of this big house. The pipe is only so big, and as the system empties, the pressure is reduced, and the flow rate slows."

Nobody said it, but they all thought it. A few hours was too long. The temperature was dropping, and some of the pipes would likely freeze before the system was empty.

Nurse brought the coffee, and they drank in silence. After only a few sips, Shorty abruptly set his cup aside and left. In a few minutes he was back, carrying several gallons of antifreeze.

Regent didn't want to show his ignorance, so he didn't ask what it was for.

"You hold my flashlight and come with me, Professor. Show me where the bathrooms are."

They began on the third floor. At the first bathroom, Shorty poured some antifreeze into the sink.

"This is a good one to start with," he said. It was against the north wall of the house, and the temperature in the room was already almost freezing.

Regent swallowed his pride and asked, "What's the point of the antifreeze? Doesn't it just run into the sewer?"

"Some does. Some stops in the traps and replaces standing water."

Shorty flushed the toilet several times, putting a little antifreeze in it each time, until the feed line was empty and the tank refused to fill again. They repeated the same procedure throughout the house.

Back in the boiler room, the situation was little changed. Emil looked at his watch.

"The first zone is probably about half-empty, but this is taking too long," he said. He pulled the hose a little way out of the drain, and the three of them looked at the stream of water. No one spoke for several minutes.

Then Emil said, "I wonder what happened to Scap?"

"Probably moving slow," Shorty said. "He's got to be tired. He brought in the last of the firewood before he left."

They fell back into silence as the water continued to gurgle into the drain. Regent had put on a wool scarf when he was upstairs making the antifreeze rounds. He fluffed it up on his neck. He pulled his stocking cap down to meet it. The three men stood quietly in the eerie flashlight illumination, their gloved hands tucked under their arms for warmth.

"I'll be back in a minute," Regent said. "Can I get you guys some extra clothes? Sweaters? Anything?"

"No thanks. These insulated coveralls will do it," Shorty said.

Regent found Nurse in a bedroom with her back to a fireplace. She looked warm and comfortable. So long as the fire lasted and she had the energy to keep turning around in front of it like meat on a spit, she would remain so.

"How about a sweater, Nurse? And a cap? Another pair of heavy socks? Might as well be prepared. We're out of wood."

He didn't say it, but he thought about how, even if the power came on immediately, it would take hours to refill the heating system and warm up the house again. They were going to be very cold before it was all over.

"The cap and extra socks sound like a good idea," she said. "And I'll wrap up in a blanket."

Better use two or three, Regent thought.

"You seen Scap?" he asked.

"He left about a quarter of an hour ago. Didn't say where he was going, just that he wouldn't be gone long." They heard footsteps on the porch. "That must be him now," Nurse said.

It wasn't. It was Nurse's nephew Ferdie. He was carrying two kerosene heaters, called Aladdins.

Regent had used Aladdins before and liked them. They put out a good deal of heat, and you could move them around while they were on.

"Evening, Professor."

Regent didn't answer.

Ferdie went on. "Cold night, isn't it? I hear it may be late tomorrow before power's restored."

Regent still didn't say anything.

"I thought you could use these heaters. I've got some more, too, if you want them. I've had them since that last ice storm a few years ago. Some extra kerosene, too. I was sort of in the emergency heating business then, you know."

Regent didn't know, but he could imagine. Ferdie had been one of those profiteering ghouls who prey on other people's misfortunes. He'd probably stolen the heaters in the first place, then sold them at exorbitant prices to desperate homeowners.

"So how much do you want for them?" Regent asked. "$500? $1000?"

"Aw, you misjudge me, Professor. They're free. I'm just trying to be a good neighbor. I don't want any money."

Regent blew air through his lips making a sound that indicated he was not at all interested in buying a bridge in Brooklyn.

"No, really. I've got some of these things going in my house, and it's warm as can be over there, even my old

Auntie's empty room. And since I had these extra heaters, I thought you could use them."

He said again, "I don't want any money."

"Well, what do you want?" Regent knew the answer.

He glanced over his shoulder and saw Nurse at the top of the stairs. She was carrying the little bag she had arrived with. She had on her coat and gloves.

"I think you know, Professor. It's time for Aunt to come home. That's all. Now, open the door and let me set up these heaters for you. They *will* keep your pipes from freezing."

"She's not here," Regent said.

"She's not here? Then who is that old lady I've been seeing in your parlor the last few days?" He smiled an ugly smile of triumph.

Louder and more firmly, Regent said, "She's not here."

"These heaters really work well, Professor..."

"She's not here." This time he shouted.

Nurse tried to push past him, but he got a firm grip on her arm so that she couldn't.

The three of them stood staring at each other in silence for a moment, each waiting to see what the others would do. Ferdie was first to act. He turned on his heel and headed back out into the snow.

"I'll be back, Professor," Ferdie yelled as he retreated. "You can count on it. I'll be back to get that old woman out of what's left of your broken-down house."

Nurse tried to wriggle free of Regent's grip.

"Let me go, Professor. There's no reason to let your house freeze up just so an old lady can have a little liberty."

Regent was not a physically demonstrative man, but he put his arm around her shoulder and pulled her to him.

"Just be quiet, will you. This is how it's going to be."

It was hard enough to watch his house being destroyed without having to argue with an old woman.

"Put that blanket around you and sit here by the fire," he commanded. "You must be tired."

She did as he said.

He left her there and took the steps to the boiler room two at a time. He didn't look the least bit tired and not at all old.

CHAPTER SEVENTEEN

Regent Solves One Problem

In the boiler room, a cabinet full of fuses and electrical connections was open. Wires hung from it like it had been vandalized.

Emil and Shorty were sitting on stools saying nothing. Regent leaned against a wall, and the three of them listened to the water flow into the drain.

Regent wanted to ask why they had torn up the fuse box, but he didn't like showing his ignorance. They must have had their reasons. He also wanted to ask if they could think of anything else that could be done to save the place. But he didn't like the rather pitiful sound of that. He joined them in silence.

At length, Shorty said, "Maybe Scap'll bring some donuts."

"That'd be good," Emil responded.

"Thought he'd be back by now," Shorty said.

"Me too," Emil said. "But you can't get good help anymore," he added, grinning.

"He's getting pretty old to be out there stomping

around in all that snow," Shorty responded.

"Yeah he is. Gotta be over 80. Tough, though. Really tough."

"Good thing he is. No telling how far he had to go. He should've skied."

Regent didn't much care where Scap had gone, but in a small effort to be civil, he asked, "Where'd he go, anyway?"

"Fire Department," Shorty said.

"What for? Is the house on fire now—even as it's freezing solid?"

The men didn't take his question seriously enough to answer it.

Regent looked at one then the other and waited. He asked again.

"What for?"

"You really *aren't* from around here, are you?" Emil said. "I'd heard that, but I didn't know you came from that far away."

"I'm from the moon," Regent said sharply. He was afraid, and he was very tired. It was affecting his manners.

Shorty sighed and said, "The Volunteer Fire Department has a couple of portable generators. They go around and supply power temporarily to the houses and buildings that are in the most trouble. When Scap finds those guys—the phone lines are down, and right now cell phones are even less dependable than usual—when he finds them, he'll get them to come by here. They'll have to plow the hill, and the way the snow is piling up, that'll take a while, but it shouldn't be too much longer."

"I don't understand," Regent said. "What good is a little power going to do, if there's no water in the system?"

The two men glanced at each other.

Shorty sighed and said, "Unless Scap dies of old age first, you'll still have some water in the system when they get here. As you can see, it takes a long time to drain. When they get here, we'll connect the generator there"—he pointed at the box with the wires hanging out—"and get the partial system working for long enough to buy a little time. That'll let us drain a little more before it freezes up, then..."

He broke off and cocked his head. "I thought I heard something."

Regent went upstairs to see. It wasn't Scap. It was Preston Butcher, the lawyer he'd met at the library. He was in the parlor talking with Nurse.

"I believe you know Preston," she said to Regent.

"Yeah, he was telling me this morning how peaceful former monasteries are," Regent said dryly.

"Everything under control here, Professor?" Butcher asked. Regent grunted sardonically.

"You've got Shorty and Emil helping out, so you should be all right. They know their stuff.

"Well, I'll be going now. I was passing by, so I thought I'd stop and see how you were doing. It was an unexpected pleasure to find Nurse here." He smiled at her. "She and I go way back.

"Thanks for the coffee," he said to her. "I'll be in touch."

He pulled on his coat and hat and started for the door.

"Don't worry, Professor. You're going to be all right."

Regent grunted again, "Maybe. Maybe not.

"Hey, there was something I wanted to ask you about this morning, but things got going a little too fast when the power went off."

Butcher pulled on his gloves and waited.

In a low voice, he said, "Since you and Nurse know each other, you may be acquainted with her problems with her nephew."

Butcher nodded.

Regent looked around at Nurse who was still in the parlor. He picked up his fur hat off a table by the door and urged Butcher into the unheated vestibule, which served as a kind of halfway house between the severe outdoor temperature and the normally warm interior. There they could talk without Nurse hearing.

Regent put his hands under his armpits and said, "She's more or less a prisoner at Ferdie's, you know."

Butcher waited.

"Ferdie can't be bothered to work, and so he depends on Nurse's little social security checks and whatever other income she might have. If she goes somewhere else to live, he'll lose it. So—it's cold out here, I'll say it quickly—is there anything that can be done legally to get her free from him?"

"Practically speaking, not much. And now that he knows she's here, I think you can expect some papers to be served before long, followed by a commitment hearing, and so forth."

"But she's not crazy, and she's not senile."

"No, she's not. But satisfying a court of that could be a little difficult."

"Why? That's not fair." He realized he sounded like a whining child.

"You're right. It's not fair, but you see, her medical history will come up, and it's a problem."

"What are you talking about?"

"A long time ago, when she was a nurse here at Franklin Manor, she took a sick child home to live with her when the little girl's family fell on hard times and could no longer meet the expense of keeping the child here. After a couple of months, she died. Nurse became very depressed. It was what's called situational depression or something like that. Not the chronic kind that is so hard to deal with. In any case, she was institutionalized for it. In time, she came to terms with her loss and was released. Myself, I have difficulty thinking of it as a medical problem. It was just extreme grief. In any case, it will all come up as a history of mental illness, if Ferdie wants to have her forcibly committed."

"Is there anything we can do?"

"There is, but I doubt you'll want to."

"Try me." Regent was feeling angry as well as cold.

"You can become her guardian."

Without hesitation, Regent said, "Oh. Well, let's do it."

"Like marriage, it's not a state to be entered into lightly.

I'll be glad to explain it all to you when we get a chance, but right now we're about to freeze to death."

Regent opened the door into the house, which, though not as warm as usual, was more comfortable than the vestibule, and it seemed quite welcoming. He took Butcher's arm and pulled him toward the dwindling parlor fire.

"Nurse, I've decided to adopt you. Is that OK with you? That way, Ferdie will never bother you again."

"Not adopt," Butcher said. "Become her guardian."

"I prefer 'adopt.'" Regent said grinning.

She looked at him without speaking.

Butcher said, "I've explained to the Professor that it involves more than he's probably aware of. And..."

Regent interrupted. "I know, I know, 'marry in haste, repent at leisure' or whatever the expression is. But tell me this, Counselor. Isn't it important to get this done before Ferdie starts making trouble?"

"That would be better, yes."

"Then draw up the papers, man," Regent said. "And as soon as they're drawn, Nurse, I'll help you move to wherever you want."

Nurse said nothing. Butcher said nothing. It was as if things were moving along too quickly to allow the formation of sentences.

Nurse was on her way to freedom. Butcher was relegated to helper status. Regent was being calmly masterful. All in an instant.

"Or, if you prefer," Regent backtracked, "you're welcome to stay here."

She cocked her old head a little to one side and looked confused.

"As long as you like," he added.

He felt like he was two people; one speaking, the other listening. Where had those words come from?

Nurse's mouth hung open and her eyes filled with tears.

Regent would have none of that. "It's the tea, Nurse."

"What?"

"The tea. You brew a fine cup of tea."

She hugged him like a young lover.

CHAPTER EIGHTEEN

More Help

Butcher hadn't been gone long, when Regent saw the lights of the fire truck plowing its way up the hill. On its grill was a fir wreath decorated with a wide red ribbon. When the scraping stopped, the sound of Bing Crosby singing "White Christmas" came out of the truck, climbed over the white berms along the sides of the street, and spread out over the ever-deepening snow.

"Firefighters with a sense of irony," Regent muttered.

Scap climbed down out of the truck. His movements weren't exactly nimble, but he didn't look his age either.

"Merry Christmas," the first firefighter said from behind his scarf. He held out a mittened hand to Regent.

"Merry Christmas to you," Regent said heartily. "This electricity you've brought is what I asked Santa for."

"Well, you must've been a good boy. We'll have you

fixed up before long."

Regent closed his eyes and felt gratitude and relief wash over him. He realized, too, that he was very tired.

The firefighters made their way up the driveway paying out electrical cable behind them.

"Right here," Scap said. With his hands he raked back snow from one of the ground-level windows in the boiler room. He banged on the glass and shouted, "Hey, Emil, open up."

When the boiler was roaring again, The men gathered around it like it was a campfire, holding out their hands to its warmth.

"How much water you got left?" a fireman asked.

"Two zones and part of a third," Shorty answered. "This house is so big, it takes a long time for all that water to run out."

They all nodded knowingly.

"Some of the radiators should be warming up pretty soon," someone said.

"Yep. Won't take long," someone else answered.

Nurse made still more coffee. They sipped and waited.

"I thought you were going to bring donuts," Emil said to Scap.

"I don't know why you thought that. The grocery store is nothing but bare shelves now. Donuts were probably the first thing to go."

Emil said, "Professor, why don't you go see if any of the radiators are getting warm yet. I don't know how the zones are laid out, so you'll have to check them all."

At the rear of the first floor, the warmth was already apparent. On the second floor, immediately above that part of the house, the radiators were just beginning to feel warm. The rooms where they were located were cold, as was the whole of the third floor.

Regent went back to the boiler room and reported what he'd found.

"Another twenty minutes and we'll have to go," one of the firemen said. "We'll get back when we can, but it'll be a while."

The whole house felt slightly warmer when they disconnected and went on their way. Nobody was taking off sweaters and hats, but the small improvement was apparent, and it made them all feel a little more cheerful.

Shorty and Emil restarted the flow of water down out of the building and into the drain.

"That should run OK," Shorty said. "Let's go have a look."

Once again Regent failed to understand what they were up to, and once again he was reluctant to admit it to them by asking. He followed them out of the room.

Some of the overhead pipes in the basement were covered by the drop ceiling, but many were out in the open. Shorty and Emil played their flashlights on the ones that they could see and followed them into the next rooms.

"Professor, you probably should do this too."

"Do what?"

"Go upstairs and see if there are any leaks."

"Leaks?"

"Yeah. These old brass pipes don't like going from hot to cold to hot the way we're making them do. I'll be surprised if there aren't places where they've popped open."

Regent closed his eyes and waited a moment for control to return. *I must be like brass pipe, myself,* he thought. *This emotional hot and cold is about to make me break.*

"Here's one," Shorty said from a storage room at the rear of the basement. "Bring a bucket, Professor."

Water was pouring from a joint at a rate that was only a little slower than it was going into the boiler room drain.

"This is a good place for a leak," Shorty said as he placed the bucket under the flow. "Won't hurt this concrete floor. What you don't want is a leak inside a wall or a plaster ceiling like we had the other day."

No kidding, Regent thought.

"Better go upstairs now, Professor, and see if there are any problems up there."

There were. On one side of the sheetrocked ceiling of the living room was a dark, sagging ring.

"OK, here's what we do about that," Emil said. He stood on a chair, and using his pocketknife, he poked holes at several points inside the discolored area. Water gushed out. "That'll keep it from building up and bringing the whole ceiling down."

Nurse had followed them with more buckets and a mop.

"How is it you have so many buckets, Professor?"

"I don't know. The nuns had them."

"Lucky for you they did," Emil said. "This is not a good time to go out looking for more. But then this house always has been charmed."

"You'll understand if I'm having a hard time seeing its charm just now," Regent said. "It's almost Christmas Eve, and the place is about to freeze solid. If not that, it's going to be destroyed by water damage. No telling what it's going to give me for a Christmas present."

The two men and Nurse and Scap looked at each other as if trying to decide who was going to respond. In the end, no one did.

After a while, Emil said, "Let's go check the rest of the house."

They found one more leak. They wrapped it with duct tape and left a bucket to catch the remaining drips.

"That's a relief," Emil said. "I was afraid we were going to find something serious."

If there had been enough light, Regent's face would have revealed the resentment he was feeling. He wished they would just keep their vapid cheerfulness to themselves. They didn't understand anything about his situation—not anything at all—not what he had hoped for from the old house, not how it was impossible to sell it without losing everything he'd invested. But in the dim light his feelings didn't show.

After a few hours, the fire department guys reappeared and stayed long enough to warm the water in the one zone that wasn't yet empty.

Then, shortly after they left, a sudden cheer erupted from the village and came sliding up over the snow and into every corner and crevice of Franklin Manor. The power was back on. Instantly, lights shone from almost every house. Christmas trees and outdoor decorations seemed brighter than anyone had ever seen. Here and there under streetlights, people jumped up and down and improvised little dances.

Shorty and Emil quickly reconnected the house to the power grid. With that, its lights came on, the refrigerator began to hum, and the boiler came to life.

"Time for us to go, Professor," Shorty said.

"Hang on a minute," Regent said. "Let's have a drink before you leave." He hurried to the pantry for the bottle and glasses.

"No ice for me," Emil called after him.

"Me either," Shorty said chuckling. "Had enough of that."

Regent raised his glass. "Thank you all. Thank you very much. I wouldn't have gotten through this without you." They drank.

After a pause, Regent added, "And you know what else?" He had some trouble getting it out. "Because you came and helped me this way, even if the house had frozen solid, I would have been able to handle it better, you know, not been so, uh—so defeated."

"Well, now you know," Scap said to Regent.

"Know what?"

"The power of the bell," Scap said.

The good will Regent had been feeling suddenly disappeared. He felt good, but he didn't feel like being preached at. He kept his manners though.

"If you say so," he responded grudgingly.

Scap wouldn't let it go. "I'm glad you decided to ring it, Professor. I wasn't sure you were going to. You were so skeptical."

Regent felt his neck grow hot, and it wasn't from the whisky.

"What are you talking about, Scap? I didn't ring the bell."

"Well somebody did. That's what brought us here," Shorty said.

Regent stared at him in puzzlement.

"I thought the nuns were back," Emil said.

"I didn't ring it," Regent said again. "I'm not even sure where it is."

"It's in the parlor," Nurse said. "I rang it."

CHAPTER NINETEEN

Out of the Past

When Regent woke the next morning it was either the second or the third day of uninterrupted snow. It might have been the fourth. He wasn't sure. In any case, he woke feeling anything but the Christmas spirit, even though it was Christmas Eve. He was quite tired, and his body was stiff from the hard work of dealing with the power outage.

He started the coffee maker and went around the house one more time looking for trouble spots. As he did, he reflected that not only was the house more trouble than ever, but now he was about to become the guardian of a person he hardly even knew. He'd even invited her to move in with him and stay as long as she wanted. What could he have been thinking? Some might attribute his rashness to the Christmas spirit. Maybe so, but in that one act he must have used it all up. He sure didn't have any left this morning.

"Good morning, Professor," Shorty and Emil said more or less together as they clomped down the back stairs into the basement. They carried tool bags, a length of pipe, and some fittings.

"Uh, good morning," Regent said. "I wasn't expecting you." He wanted to add, "Doesn't anyone ever knock before entering my house?" but he didn't.

"We thought you might still be asleep, so we just let ourselves in. Wanted to get an early start so we can get home to our families."

"Early start doing what?"

"Fixing those leaks," Shorty said a little impatiently.

"Why are you guys doing all this anyway?" Regent asked. "You don't even know me. I don't get it."

"It's the bell," Shorty said. "When it rings—well, you know."

Regent had no response. He watched them work for a while, in hopes of learning something about plumbing. He was too tired for it though, so he went upstairs to shower and dress.

When he came back down, they were gone. The buckets were stacked neatly in the boiler room, and there were shiny new pieces of copper pipe and fittings where the leaks had been.

With that, Regent's spirits rose as high as his fatigue would permit.

He put on his boots and hat and all the usual cold

weather gear, walked out into the deepest snow he'd ever seen, and started slogging toward the grocery store. Had he still been alone in the house, he probably would have been satisfied with the sardines and crackers that were about all he had on hand. But with Nurse to care for, that wouldn't do. Anyway, it wasn't but half a mile or so.

The streets of the little downtown area were crowded with pedestrians and cars—people doing last-minute Christmas shopping.

Regent viewed the scene from a block or so away, where his route to the grocery store passed at the high end of a hill block. He was happy to have it that way. The holiday activity was interesting from a distance, but he didn't feel like participating.

"Spare change, Sir?"

Distracted by the bustle, he had almost bumped into a woman standing in the narrow path. Not young, not old, she kept her head down and held out a threadbare mittened hand.

Had he been paying attention instead of looking down toward Main Street, he would have crossed the street in order to avoid her. He didn't like to say no, and he didn't like to say yes. He didn't like to have such encounters at all.

He pulled off a glove, reached into his pocket, and gave her the coins he found there.

"Thank you and Merry Christmas," she said.

"Uh, yeah," he said uncomfortably, "same to you."

He found her less repellant than most panhandlers. She

didn't seem drugged out. She didn't have a stud in her tongue or a tattoo on her neck. And even though she'd spoken but a few words, her language somehow seemed less unrefined than he expected.

He took a chance. "Can you tell me something please? How did it come to this?"

She said nothing for a moment. It was hard to imagine that she had not already thought long and hard about it. The pause seemed designed for dramatic effect, something an actress would do.

"It just did," she said, and abruptly she clambered over the snow bank and started across the street. As she did, a slow-moving car came around the corner and went a little out of control on a patch of ice. In seconds, she was underneath the front bumper and buried in deep snow at Regent's feet.

She was conscious but not very. Regent squatted and carefully slipped his scarf under her head. A crowd gathered quickly, and some of them pushed the car back into the street. Others gathered around the woman in a little circle.

"Where does it hurt?" Regent asked.

"It's nothing," she said.

The car had slowed by the time it made impact, and the snow had cushioned her fall. Even so, it didn't seem like "nothing."

"Lie still. EMS will be here very soon."

"Just let me catch my breath. I don't need EMS." She

struggled to stand up, but he gently restrained her.

"Be still for a moment until the shock wears off. Then see how you feel."

She took deep breaths and did what he told her.

"What's your name?"

She didn't answer.

"What day is this?"

"Christmas Eve, of course."

"Where do you live?"

"Let it alone, Professor Regent."

His head popped back like he'd been punched. "How do you know my name?"

At that point her eyelids fluttered a little, and she lost consciousness. A moment later, the EMTs arrived. In the woman's pocket, one of them found a thin wallet. He said to his partner, "Jane Felsher Kravitz, Roanoke, Virginia. Wonder what she's doing up here?"

The adrenaline rush Regent had experienced when the accident occurred had been about to subside, but when he heard the name, it came back with more force than ever. He looked at her more closely. She'd grown older and added some lines to her face, but she was indeed Jane Felsher Kravitz.

"I want to go with you," he said to the EMTs. "It turns out I know her. Just hadn't recognized her."

On the ride to the hospital, he recalled what he knew about Jane. It had been about ten years since he'd last seen her. She'd been his student—a very good one—just at the time when he was becoming terminally disenchanted with teaching. She'd wanted to be a writer.

He had counseled her in the usual way. It was an impractical ambition. Better have a way to make a living while waiting to be published.

She responded in the usual way. "I want to write full time, not in the evening after I come home from some job I don't like."

The last time he'd seen her, she was leaving campus to go to her mother's funeral. She hadn't returned.

"Professor Regent?" a clerk called. He stood up and was shown into an examining room. Jane was lying on a gurney. An IV drip was attached to her arm.

"Hello, Jane."

"See what happens when you give money to street people?" she said.

He smiled and said, "I'm glad to see you again, Jane, but I don't care much for the circumstances."

"Don't worry. I'm not hurt. This bag of glucose is just my Christmas dinner. As soon as it's finished, I'm out of here."

He bit back the questions he wanted to ask.

A physician assistant came into the room and adjusted the drip.

"Feeling better?" he asked.

"Yes, thanks."

"Well, let me say it again. You can leave if you must, but it would be better if you stayed for a day or two."

She shook her head back and forth the whole time he speaking, but it didn't slow him down.

"You need food and rest. And the snow is supposed to continue for some time yet."

"Thank you for your concern, but as soon as that bag is empty, I'm out of here."

The PA turned to Regent and asked, "Who are you?"

"Butch Regent, a friend."

"Do you know where Ms. Kravitz lives? She won't tell us."

"No, I don't, but I can guess." He turned to her. "Jane, you're living on the street, aren't you?"

She didn't respond. All three of them were silent for a while.

"How about we do this," Regent said. He hoped his voice wasn't showing the reluctance he felt.

"You come home with me for a few days, Jane. It happens I have a registered nurse in residence. And somewhere around sixteen bedrooms."

The toughness that had been the woman's most prominent feature so far melted like the snow on her boots.

After Regent had gotten Jane into the house and introduced her to Nurse, the EMTs dropped him at the grocery store.

When he returned to Franklin Manor with a frozen pizza and a sweater and toilet articles for Jane, darkness had fallen.

It was that point on Christmas Eve when children begin to find the wait for Santa almost unbearable.

CHAPTER TWENTY

The Night Before Christmas

If they hadn't been so tired, they might have spent the evening in some semblance of happy Christmas Eve conversation. As it was, they just chatted a little between yawns, ate the insipid grocery store pizza, and turned in early.

Before crawling into his sleeping bag, Regent looked down from his cure porch. It was still snowing heavily, but he was able to make out Christmas lights twinkling below. The sound of carols drifted up from the village.

A young girl walked slowly up the hill on the street in front. She stopped a moment, coughed violently, looked up at the house, then disappeared from sight behind the cedar trees at the edge of the property.

"A beautiful evening, isn't it Maalox," Regent said half-aloud. He could almost feel the dog's tail thumping in agreement.

Before the bag even began to get warm, he was sleeping soundly. He was very tired, and besides that he felt at peace in a way that was unusual for him, especially during the past few years.

His quiet sleep didn't last long. Somebody was having a party, and its sound filled his porch.

He unzipped the bag and emerged into the frigid air. The neighbors' houses were dark and quiet, but light was pouring from his own ground-floor windows. It reflected off the falling snow.

Despite being groggy with sleep, he still had the good feeling that had been with him at bedtime. Worse things could happen than having a Christmas party. He pulled on wool pants, a good sweater, and a tweed jacket. On the way out, he stopped before the mirror and brushed his thin, gray hair.

Midway down the stairs, he stopped. The party spread out before him in a Christmas-card tableau.

Great fires were roaring on every hearth. Any number of people dressed in their Christmas best were laughing and eating and having a fine time. The big dining room that had been empty of furniture when he'd gone to bed a couple of hours earlier now had several round banquet tables in it. One held a punch bowl and glasses and canapés and bottles of champagne. Another, a turkey and a ham and vegetables. A third, pies and fruitcake and custard.

In a corner of the living room, people were gathered around a grand piano singing "Good King Wenceslas."

Regent was humming along under his breath when Sister Julia spotted him. She fairly danced up the stairs and kissed him enthusiastically.

"Merry Christmas, Professor. Merry Christmas."

"Merry Christmas to you, Sister. What a grand party."

"Oh, isn't it though?"

She hooked her arm through his and escorted him down into the living room. As they entered, the guests stopped singing and talking and burst into applause.

"What is all this, Sister? I don't understand it at all. I like it, but I don't understand it."

"These dear ones are saying welcome, that's all. Let's get you a glass of champagne."

He drank gratefully, and took a moment to observe the guests more closely. Some were wearing clothes that hadn't been fashionable for decades.

"What's with the Halloween costumes, Sister?"

"They aren't costumes, but it is a Halloween party in a way. You know, All Saints, that sort of thing..." She left it in the air for him to figure out.

She took him across the room and introduced him to four nuns in old-fashioned habits.

"So nice to see you here, Professor," one of them said. "We've been a bit worried about you. Weren't sure you'd make it." The other nuns nodded agreement.

"You look familiar, Sister," he said. "Have we met before?"

All four of them giggled as if they might have had a bit too much champagne.

"Not in a way you'd remember," Sister said merrily.

Then it came to him. Sister Frances. He'd seen her in a photograph. She was famous for her "peaceful passing." "Died sitting in a rocking chair in the St. Joseph Room. Utterly serene."

He took a big gulp of champagne and tried to form the question.

"Come with me," Sister Julia said. She pulled him into a quiet corner.

"Sister Frances is—uh—dead," Regent said.

"That's right. So are the other three." She paused a moment. "Most of the guests are."

Regent thought he should be afraid or nervous or something like that. But he wasn't.

"Shall we have another glass of bubbly?" he asked.

"Yes, let's do," Sister Julia said, "and then I'll introduce you to the other guests."

She motioned to a man who had gray muttonchop whiskers and wore a wing collar and a long out-of-date suit. He was clearly older than either of the young women on his arm. They had short hair and wore the short skirts and turned-down hose of flappers.

"Merry Christmas, Professor." The man stuck out his hand. "Reginald Akers. These gorgeous young women are May and Lola, friends of mine from the adjacent porch. We played lots of whist together when we were in this house. Happy times we had. At first we were almost consumed with fear, but then we made an agreement. If we had to die, we had to die, but we didn't have to die until we actually did die, if you know what I mean."

Regent said that he thought he did know.

Suddenly, from near the big window that overlooked the floodlit back yard, someone announced in a loud, theatrical voice, "They're here." The guests went suddenly quiet and crowded toward the window.

A moose and her calf were coming through the back gate. Beyond them, two black bears and several deer could be seen dimly through the falling snow. A pileated woodpecker landed in the hollow of an ancient sugar maple. A pine marten clambered up the trunk. Soon the yard was crowded with animals.

And jumping through the deep snow like he was going over ocean breakers was Maalox.

Regent ran to the door as fast as his strained old body would move and met the dog on the back steps. Man and dog fell in the snow and wrestled around ecstatically. Everyone clapped and smiled and wiped their eyes.

Upon entering, Maalox shook the snow from his coat, covering the walls and the professor and everyone nearby with a fine spray.

"You haven't changed a bit," Regent said, a great smile lighting up his old face.

He gave Maalox a thick slice of ham, which he gulped down as he made his way to the hearth where he turned around several times in a tight circle, collapsed on the warm bricks, sighed deeply, and fell into a peaceful sleep.

Regent petted his head and said, "You're a good dog, Maalox. You're a good dog." Without opening his eyes, Maalox thumped his tail a couple of times.

Regent looked up at Sister Julia and made a sweeping gesture that encompassed the guests both indoors and out. "Are these the angels you told me about, Sister? They must be. Maalox is one. That I know."

Sister Julia didn't answer, and Regent reflected a moment before continuing. "I suppose they died here in peace and without reproach, and even in death they cannot leave this special place. Is that how it works?"

All heads nodded and every face took on a Christmas wreath of a smile.

"But what are you doing here, Sister? You're not dead. And I see Nurse and Scap over there. Emil and Shorty, too. They're sure not dead."

"Sorry to be late," Preston Butcher called from the doorway. He brushed snow off his coat and stamped his boots. "This took a while." He held up a thick manila envelope. "Merry Christmas, everyone."

"Hello, Counselor. Merry Christmas," Regent said.

He turned back to Sister Julia and repeated the question.

"Explain to me, Sister, how it's possible that you and I and our friends are here with these angels."

"It's not a thing to be explained, Professor. It's not about understanding."

"No?"

"No. It's about being."

Then she rapped a fork on the side of her glass and moved to the front of the fireplace, taking care not to step on Maalox.

"It's my great pleasure to speak on behalf of all of us, Professor, and to welcome you to the annual Franklin Manor Christmas party."

Sister Julia and all the guests raised their glasses. "To you, Professor Regent. May you join us here next year and the next and so long as Christmas brings the promise of peace.

"Now Susan has a gift for you."

He hadn't noticed her until now. "Susan" was seven-year-old Beatrice Karen Susan Cooper.

"Well," he said. "Well. You told me there was going to be this party, Susan, but I didn't believe you."

"I know," she said, rolling her eyes a little, as was her custom.

"Now see here," he began crossly. He didn't get far, though, before he saw that she was teasing.

He also saw that Susan and Nurse were holding hands.

"Of course," he said, smacking his forehead with his palm. "You were the child Nurse took home to care for and—"

"That's right, Professor," Nurse said. "Christmas is such a wonderful time, isn't it?"

"And you're not coughing, Susan," Regent said.

"No, no," Nurse said. "The cough was because she showed up early for the party. She's always been a little naughty."

"The gift, Susan," Sister Julia prompted.

"All right," the girl said. "Professor Regent, Nurse wants you to have this gift to help you with your plans for Franklin Manor." She handed him the envelope that Butcher had brought.

Inside it Regent found a legal document. He started to read but quickly got bogged down in the details.

"What is this, Preston?" he asked.

"It's an instrument that names you as beneficiary of a trust for your use in completing the renovation of Franklin Manor and establishing the artists' colony that you've been thinking of. It's a gift from Nurse."

Regent fumbled for a way to form the question. "From Nurse? But Nurse doesn't—a trust?"

"One of the men she took to cure at her house recovered and later became very wealthy. He left her a great deal of money," Butcher said.

"That explains Ferdie's behavior," Regent said.

"Yes. But thanks to you, there'll be no more of that," Butcher said.

"I can't believe this. I can really have my dream for this house?"

"Believe it, Professor," Butcher said. "Believe it."

Regent went on, rapt with the vision. "Friends living together here. Reading, talking..." He broke off and for a while went far, far away into a life yet to come.

"And as for myself—can it be? No more beating myself up for past failures? Can it be?"

"We found such peace here," someone said. All around, there was an enthusiastic murmur of agreement. Maalox barked and thumped his tail on the hearth. The creatures in the back yard nodded heads and flapped wings saying that it had existed in this place even before the house was built.

"You've already got a start on such a life, if I'm any judge of it," Butcher said. "With Nurse here indefinitely, and your new, old friend, Ms. Kravitz, you've got a good start."

"Yes I do," Regent said. "Yes I do. And you know, I was thinking just the other day that if I were to find the means to form such a household, I wouldn't do it like the usual artists' colony, where people have to qualify for admission on the basis of artistic accomplishment and promise. I'd just bring in interesting people who are skilled at conversation and are good company—maybe some would love books and music like I do—and we'd simply share our lives here in this special house.

"You are right, Preston, I certainly do have a start on that."

Then, for the first time, Regent noticed a very big Christmas tree standing in the curve of the bow windows. It had lights of every color, but all the ornaments were identical—little brass bells exactly like the one Liam Flanagan had given him.

Suddenly, all the guests—quick and dead alike—cried

out softly in wonder, for quite abruptly, the snow had stopped falling. And at the same moment, the bells began to move back and forth, slowly at first, then picking up speed. Soon they filled the old house with a sweet, tinkling choir of sound that spread a spell of Christmas peace over all who had ears to hear.

Standing by the tree smiling broadly was Liam Flanagan.

CHAPTER TWENTY-ONE

Christmas Day

Next morning, Regent slept late. It was already daylight when he pulled himself out of his down bag and hurried into the warm house. The snow had stopped, the sky was as blue as a sky could be, and light was reflecting off the snow intensely. It was a picture-perfect Christmas morning. Even Regent recognized it.

He tested his responses and inventoried his feelings as he dressed.

Beautiful day. Good.

Tired. Not good. Hard to understand too, since he'd turned in early.

Sore as a young athlete after a big game. Bad, but understandable. Could be worse.

Uncharacteristically cheerful. A Christmas mystery.

In the kitchen, Nurse and Jane were chatting and drinking coffee. Bach's *Christmas Oratorio* was on the radio.

"Merry Christmas, Professor," they said almost in unison.

"Merry Christmas, ladies."

How odd, he thought. *It's quite a nice thing to have them here, even though they have taken over my kitchen.*

"How do you feel, Jane? You don't look like you got run over yesterday."

"Creaky, but that's all. Ibuprofen is an effective drug, especially in large doses and when combined with this wonderfully quiet house. I slept very soundly."

"We waited for you to come down before starting breakfast, Professor," Nurse said. "We were thinking about making pancakes, eggs, and sausage. Does that suit?"

"It sounds wonderful. I'm very hungry." He stretched and yawned. "Don't know why, but I don't feel very rested this morning. I certainly slept long enough."

"The important thing is did you sleep well," Jane said. "You know, some sleep is more restful than other sleep."

"Yeah, pretty well. I did have a funny dream though. Can't remember it clearly. Something about a Christmas party. Went on for a long time."

Nurse smiled.

"I wonder what's wrong with me," Jane said. "I didn't dream at all."

"Too tired probably," Regent said. "What do you think, Nurse?"

"Probably."

To Jane she said, "Rest. Eat. Get to feeling better.

Dreams come when they're ready to come."

Over the pancakes and eggs, Regent said, "When I was a child, I'd already be outside by this time. Old habits die hard, I guess, because I'd like to go outside now. Sort of see what the other kids got for Christmas, know what I mean?"

The women nodded in agreement.

Nurse said, "Well, it's a beautiful day, so why don't we do that?"

They left the dishes on the table and began pulling on their heavy clothes and boots.

At the corner some children were rushing toward the village sledding hill on the next block.

"You must have been good kids," Regent said. "A new sled and a toboggan, too."

"We were," one of the boys said. "Come on up to the top, and we'll let you have a ride," he teased.

"All right," Regent said enthusiastically.

He dragged the sled up the hill, and took a free-flying, exhilarating run in prone position.

"Thanks for the ride, kids, and Merry Christmas. I'll be back tomorrow for another."

Regent caught up with the ladies, and the three of them walked for half an hour or so before returning to Franklin Manor.

They took off their wraps and settled themselves in the parlor. The circumstances called for a big fire, but the wood had been used up during the power outage. Regent resisted complaining.

They drank more coffee and reread the five pages of a day-old Oliver's Mountain *Eagle*. They looked out the window from time to time. They listened to the holiday offerings on National Public Radio and cheered softly at the end of the John Henry Faulk story about a Christmas during the Depression.

They had run completely out of things to talk about and were sitting in silence when Scap crossed the porch in front of the bow windows.

Regent went eagerly to the door.

"Hello, Scap. Merry Christmas. Come in and have a cup of coffee. I wish I had something stronger to offer, but I'm afraid Nurse drank it all."

"Don't say that to him, Professor. He's a notorious gossip. Everybody in the village will think I've got a problem."

"Oh don't worry, Delia. Your secret is safe with me," Scap said merrily.

"Scap, this is my old friend, Jane. Jane, Scap."

"Hello," Jane said, through a yawn. "Nice to meet you, but I'm going to excuse myself. I need a nap."

While they drank coffee, Regent began thinking about food. There were lima beans in the freezer, some salad makings, and a bit of cold chicken. Not much of a Christmas dinner. But at least the house was warm and nothing was broken. Not at the moment anyhow.

"Scap, will you stay for dinner? It won't be anything fancy. I just didn't get it organized." *Besides being broke*, he thought. "But we won't go hungry."

"I sure will. Thank you very much," Scap said eagerly. "But, uh, Professor, if you'd like a traditional Christmas dinner with all the trimmings, I have a suggestion."

"Oh yeah? What's that?"

"No disrespect," Scap grinned, "but you're a slow learner." He paused for effect, then spoke rather more forcefully than was his custom. "RING THE BELL."

"Oh—uh—why don't you do it, Scap."

Scap didn't hesitate. He took the bell out of its box and moved it slowly back and forth. As he did, every bell in every church in the village began to ring.

Regent's mouth dropped open a little. *Just a coincidence*, he told himself; *it was noon on Christmas Day.* They sat in silence for a time.

Finally, Regent broke the spell. "Since this thing is going to get us a Christmas dinner, I hope it'll throw in some firewood and some Christmas whisky, preferably single malt."

"It could happen," Scap said.

"It could," Nurse agreed.

"Well, while we're waiting for all that good stuff to arrive, I'm going downstairs and have a go at peanut butter sandwiches and soup. Sledding makes a guy hungry."

After eating the little lunch, they went to their rooms for a nap. Scap dozed on the parlor couch.

They all woke at about the same time, and together they did the midafternoon reorientation that follows a strong nap. They walked around the house aimlessly for a bit, then regrouped in the parlor. Regent was going through drawers looking for playing cards when it happened.

Sister Julia, some people Regent didn't know, and the children he'd been sledding with came to the door. They carried any number of boxes and bags and aluminum foil containers.

"Merry Christmas, everybody," Sister Julia said. Without putting her packages down, she gave kisses all around.

"Put those things down in the kitchen," she directed her helpers.

Soon, all the counters and tables were covered with what they had brought—a magazine-cover roast turkey, mashed potatoes, a large container of giblet gravy, green beans, cranberries, and every other requirement of a by-the-book Christmas dinner.

Regent and his companions stood to one side and watched. Scap and Nurse smiled easily. Jane looked bemused. Regent was ill at ease. He didn't want to think of himself as an object of charity, and it was difficult not to.

"To what do we owe this wonderful surprise?" he asked finally.

"It's a Christmas present," Sister Julia answered. "And since you've just established yourselves as a sort of family, it's a housewarming gift, too." Something in his expression caused Sister Julia to elaborate.

"We were working at the church this morning, putting together meals for shut-ins, and a couple of hours ago— actually it was when all the bells rang out—I thought of you, that's all."

Scap and Nurse looked at each other and nodded in a way that seemed to say, "No surprise there."

Regent kept his thoughts to himself, and said only, "Well, thank you all, very much."

"You're most welcome," Sister Julia answered. "We have to go now. Merry Christmas everybody."

Regent and his little group walked them to the door and said goodbye.

"I don't know how you did it, Scap," Regent said. "Very clever, though. For a moment, I was almost a believer. If you hadn't overlooked the Scotch—single malt Scotch, by the way, and the firewood, I would have fallen for it."

Before Scap could respond, Sister Julia reappeared on the porch. "I almost forgot," she said. "Here's a bottle of something called Glenfiddich. Someone gave it to my brother, but the doctor has taken him off liquor. I'm told it's quite good."

Regent thanked her again. Scap and Nurse hid grins behind their hands.

A half-hour later, Shorty and Emil showed up with a truckload of well-seasoned firewood.

Regent grunted and shook his head.

Through much of the late afternoon they ate and talked and celebrated most amiably. Afterward, they sat in front of a don't-spare-the-firewood blaze and enjoyed the whisky.

No one had pressed the issue. And Regent had not brought it up. They just let the day's events be the day's events.

As dusk began to settle in, Regent said, "It's getting dark, Scap. Colder, too. You want me to go with you?"

"No, it's not far, and I don't have much to carry. I'll just get my toothbrush and a few things. The rest can wait."

Over fruitcake and coffee, Scap had let it be known that his room in a rundown old house had been damaged by the power outage. He was without plumbing, and they suspected he didn't have the money to move to a new place. Before coffee was poured, they had all of them, Jane included, persuaded him to join them at Franklin Manor.

"Stay as long as you like," Regent had said. Then, a wry half-smile playing briefly across his face, he added, "We can use a man with your talents."

In the evening, as Regent was passing by the door to the unfurnished living room, his eye fell on something under the bow windows. His footsteps on the maple floor echoed through the emptiness as he went over for a closer look.

He bent his long, stiff old body and picked up some of the stuff.

"Huh, what's this?" he said under his breath. "Fir needles. Still sticky with resin. Fir needles."

He shook his head and frowned in puzzlement.

Then he rejoined Nurse and Jane and Scap in the parlor and put another log on the fire.

"Well, Merry Christmas everybody."

"Merry Christmas, Professor. Merry Christmas."

THE END

Now Available

AN UNABRIDGED RECORDING OF

A Franklin Manor Christmas

read by PAUL WILLCOTT

A perfect gift.
A perfect way to spend a holiday evening.

Order online from

www.wordstruckpress.com

3 CD SET ◆ 3 HOURS

Want to spend more time at Franklin Manor with Professor Regent and his new friends?

Join them in *A Franklin Manor Epiphany* as they make a life together, and Professor Regent learns to see in a new way.

Jane comes stage-center as an accused thief, and the former monastery adds two more residents—a "writer" with a prodigous memory and an 85-year-old caretaker cat.

A Franklin Manor Epiphany

by PAUL WILLCOTT

Available in bookstores November, 2009.

Pre-order online at www.wordstruckpress.com

DESIGNED BY Karen Davidson

COPY EDITING BY Mary Thill

Typeset in the old-style-serif

Monotype Janson font family

designed by Robin Nicholas and Patricia Saunders.

Based on types originally cut by the Hungarian punch-cutter, Nicolas Kis,

circa 1690, and named after Anton Janson, a Dutch printer.

PRINTED IN THE USA BY BookMasters, Inc.

on 70# Finch opaque.